HERRESHOFF YACHTS

After the 1934 America's Cup defense, the J-class yacht *Rainbow* was laid up in dry dock for two years in Bristol, and then refitted by Vanderbilt as a trial horse. In 1937, she was sold to Chandler Hovey to race the defender selection trials, but *Ranger* eliminated her. *Rainbow* was laid up at the end of 1937 at the Herreshoff yard in Bristol and sold for scrap in 1940.

HERRESHOFF YACHTS

SEVEN GENERATIONS OF INDUSTRIALISTS, INVENTORS AND INGENUITY IN BRISTOL

RICHARD V. SIMPSON

Charleston   London

History
PRESS

Published by The History Press
Charleston, SC 29403
www.historypress.net

Cover image: Enterprise. Courtesy of the Mariners' Museum.
All images courtesy of the author unless otherwise noted.

First published 2007

Manufactured in the United Kingdom

ISBN 978.1.59629.306.9

Library of Congress Cataloging-in-Publication Data

Simpson, Richard V.
   Herreshoff yachts : seven generations of industrialists, inventors and ingenuity in Bristol / Richard V. Simpson.
      p. cm.
   Includes bibliographical references.
   ISBN-13: 978-1-59629-306-9 (alk. paper)
1. Naval architects--United States--Biography. 2. Yacht designers--United States--Biography. 3. Herreshoff family. 4. Boatbuilders--Rhode Island--Bristol (Town)--Biography. 5. Boatbuilding--Rhode Island--Bristol (Town)--History. 6. Yacht building--Rhode Island--Bristol (Town)--History.
I. Title.
   VM139.S56 2007
   338.7'623820092273--dc22
                                        2007013367

CONTENTS

FOREWORD

Richard V. Simpson herein provides a fascinating take on the notable Herreshoff story of acclaimed innovative design of power and sail craft, technical superiority and signal success in competitive yacht racing. Richard, a Bristol aficionado of the Herreshoff tradition, brings to the subject his distinguishing approach for lively presentation of historical fact based upon authorship of a dozen previous books.

Since so much factual information is already in the written record, especially commendable is Richard's choice to concentrate on previously neglected subject matter, especially the character and accomplishments of notable members of the Herreshoff family reaching back seven generations. Thus, here is not just an account of what happened, but rather of the why and how of Herreshoff domination over much of what they undertook during two centuries of design and construction of the world's finest power and sail craft, including those that defended the America's Cup eight successive times.

My brother, Nathanael G. Herreshoff III, and I have been privileged to provide consultation and assistance with family history to benefit Richard's historical record. In this way, we feel that with him we enhance the history that is the focus of the Herreshoff Marine Museum.

We are pleased to see included considerable verbatim quotation of newspaper accounts of significant accomplishments. This provides both credibility of fact and flavor of contemporary appreciations. There is further amplification by wonderful period photographs and illustrations. Altogether Richard V. Simpson affords the reader insights never before provided.

Halsey C. Herreshoff
President, Herreshoff Marine Museum/America's Cup Hall of Fame
March 2007

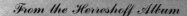

From the Herreshoff Album

First to fly the Atlantic! The famous NC-4 was the first aeroplane to fly the Atlantic Ocean. It took off from Trepassey Bay, Newfoundland, in May, 1919 . . . just 25 years ago this month. Because of our experience in building lightweight but rugged pleasure craft, the United States Navy awarded Herreshoff the contract for building the streamlined hull and pontoons for the NC-4.

THE FAMOUS NC-4 — 1919

433

OFFICIAL U. S. NAVY PHOTO

Fine Craftsmanship

. . . which for 80 years has earned international renown for Herreshoff pleasure craft, is today faithfully employed in the construction of the many high-speed Motor Torpedo Boats (PTs) which we are building for the United States Navy, and the Aircraft Rescue Boats being built by us for the Army Air Forces. Where speed and endurance are so important, the highest quality materials and workmanship are vital.

Herreshoff

SHIPYARD
BRISTOL, RHODE ISLAND

Acknowledgements

I extend special thanks to John J. Palmieri, curator of the Herreshoff Marine Museum; Halsey C. Herreshoff, president of the Herreshoff Marine Museum and America's Cup Hall of Fame; and Nathanael Greene Herreshoff III, Herreshoff family historian. These contributors aided in research, read the manuscript and offered constructive recommendations to make this book an accurate and easy to read history of America's foremost boat builder.

Particular thanks to Joseph J. Bains, a fellow collector and regional history enthusiast without whose photography talent many of the photographs in this collection would not be here.

I am grateful for being allowed access to the museum's photo archives and for the cooperation and patience of museum staff, especially archivist librarian Norene Rickson.

PHOTO — COURTESY OF HUBBARD'S SOUTH COAST CO

*First Aid
for Fliers . . .
forced down at sea!*

The lives of many of our Airmen are saved by the
high-speed, able handling, and reliable performance of
the Aircraft Rescue Boats we are building for the Army
Air Forces. Never before has the traditional Herreshoff
craftsmanship served a finer purpose.

Herreshoff

SHIPYARD
BRISTOL, RHODE ISLAND

BUY WAR BONDS

INTRODUCTION

Bristol, Rhode Island, has been engaged in various manufacturing industries during nearly the entire period of its history. The earliest manufactory of which we have knowledge is the making of malt liquors by John Cary in 1681 in his Chestnut Street brewery. As late as June 1884, Chestnut Street was still known as "Malt House Lane." This was followed by other breweries and distilleries manufacturing malt liquors and rum. These businesses survived for about one and a half centuries before they wholly ceased.

Several gristmills have operated in the town, some operated by tidal dams and some by wind power. The oldest mill of which there is a record was built by Joseph Reynolds some time prior to 1700, on Bristol Neck. After about twenty years it was moved farther south to the head of the harbor, at the place still called Windmill Point.

The state of Rhode Island is one-third tidewater. She boasts more miles of coastline than all other New England states combined, so she is quite properly called the Ocean State. Since colonial times, Rhode Island has found her fortune and character in, on and around Narragansett Bay. Rhode Island, up through the middle of the nineteenth century, was predominantly a maritime state. From the earliest times until the decline of the foreign commerce and the introduction of steam vessels, shipbuilding was a leading industry on Narragansett Bay. The vessels used in the various maritime enterprises, whether as merchantmen, whalers, slavers, privateers or shallow draft coasting vessels, were generally built in the locality from which they sailed.

For a long period, shipbuilding occupied a prominent place among the industries of Bristol, employing large numbers of men and boys. Records reveal that as early as 1696, two large merchantmen, the *Grampus* and the *Dolphin*, were built in Bristol. This industry had its greatest prosperity from 1824 to 1851; during a period of twenty-six industrious years, some sixty commercial vessels were built and rigged in Bristol.

Tax records of 1837 confirm that sixteen whalers brought cargo into the port of Bristol, and in that year Bristol's whaling fleet consisted of nineteen vessels. About 1845, Bristol's whale fishery and related sperm-oil business began to decline, and in a few years it had utterly died out. New industries such as the manufacture of rubber goods, cotton cloth, rifles, sugar and pleasure yachts were founded, prospered and faded away.

INTRODUCTION

After the shipbuilding firm of Brown & Ives of Providence, the foremost name in Rhode Island boat building is the Herreshoff Manufacturing Company of Bristol. The shipbuilding business, which had materially declined in 1856, increased when the Herreshoffs began building sailing craft in 1863, at Hope and Burnside Streets. The founding of the Herreshoff Manufacturing Company came about in 1878.

The Herreshoffs' swift schooners and sloops were their sole product for about ten years. Construction of steam-powered vessels began with the sixty-foot *Annie Morse* in 1868. Production records attest to the popularity of the Herreshoffs' steamers; twenty-eight steamers were designed, built and launched during the years from 1868 to 1876.

In 1873, the character of the business changed from sailing to steam craft. Nearly all the vessels built by this boatyard are noted for their superior construction and speed. A well-deserved international reputation and sales developed and production of fast, lightweight military vessels continued until the end of World War II.

Though the name Herreshoff has come to connote a long list of successful America's Cup defenders, dating back to the *Vigilant* in 1893, this boatyard also designed and built hundreds of pleasure craft, many of which are still being enjoyed by a new generation of owners.

Until recently, except for articles and books directed to the yachting fraternity, little has been written about the Herreshoffs as creative and resourceful individuals.

The old tannery, looking south about 1866. This is where J.B. began his boat building enterprise. *Courtesy J.J. Banes collection.*

Hope Street looking south. Seen on the left are the east shops and mold lofts; on the right are the north construction sheds.

Hope Street looking north. This building is the south construction shed.

INTRODUCTION

Herreshoff Boat Shops, Bristol, R. I.

A view of all three construction sheds from Bristol Harbor. The steel structure is the so-called shear leg, which is used to raise large masts onto boats.

As a family they are remarkably restrained, preferring to let their accomplishments go before them, as proxies, in receiving acclaim.

Hundreds of gallons of ink have been expended telling the story of the Herreshoffs' gallant sailing craft. However, there are other especially interesting tales of their lives that should be told. One is the account of the family's origin and its lineage in America; another is the story of their extraordinary inventiveness, their revolutionary steam engines, steam-driven yachts, commercial and military service vessels.

CHAPTER 1

DIVINING THE HERRESHOFF NAME

Appearing on the commentary page of the Monday, May 13, 1996 *Providence Journal*, Halsey C. Herreshoff wrote the following clarification on the pronunciation of his family name. Halsey is the grandson of Captain Nat, and he is a member of the Bristol Town Council.

> *It is quite true that the prevailing pronunciation is phonetically Herr-es-choff. However, we Herreshoffs assert that the correct pronunciation sounds like Herr-es-off, without any gratuitous supply of a nonexistent c before hoff.*
>
> *Just why the name is generally mispronounced is not clear. An example of the problem is the experience some years ago of my late uncle Clarence Herreshoff when he was an engineer at the Bureau of Ships in Washington. He placed a call to an admiral in the Pentagon and said that it was Clarence Herr-es-off calling. The admiral grumbled, "Who?" and got my uncle to repeat his name twice: Herr-es-off.*
>
> *Then a light seemed to go on in the admiral's mind: he said, "Oh you mean Herr-es-choff," and proceeded with business. Clarence said that, from that time forward, he did not much bother trying to correct people.*

The following paragraphs on the origin of the name Herreshoff are by Nathanael Greene Herreshoff III. The author taught high school German for over twenty years, and also taught German at Trenton State College, now the College of New Jersey, in their evening extension program from 1962 to 1974.

> *There are several possibilities as to the origin of the name Herreshoff. In the past the spelling of the name has appeared in several different forms, including Herreschoff and Herreschhoff. After he came to America from Prussia around 1787, Karl Friedrich Herreshoff[1] anglicized his name to Charles Frederick Herreshoff.[2] Many of his descendants have been named after him with that spelling. However, I have a son named Karl Friedrich Herreshoff born in 1963.*
>
> *Looking at the Herreshoff name in its modern form it appears to mean "lord of the court" or "lord of the farm." A grammatical spelling in modern German would be Herrenhof.*

Some sources have thought that the name was originally Eschoff with the Herr added later in front and the "c" dropped. This might indicate a Russian origin. Karl Friedrich's father was supposedly in the Prussian army. An ancestor of his might have been one of the tall Russians sent by Peter the Great in 1717 to King Friedrich Wilhelm of Prussia in exchange for the famous Amber Room.[3] Friedrich Wilhelm had a regiment of giants called "die langen kerle," which translates into English as "the tall fellows." They were all over six feet tall and recruited from all over Europe by various means.[4]

A third possible origin of the name Herreshoff is totally my own idea. It is that the name as it was spelled Herreschoff or Herreschhoff could have been originally composed of the words "Herr-Esch(e)-hof." This would translate to "lord of the (Esche) ash tree farm or court." Also, "-hoff" is used as a Westphalian place name suffix, meaning farm or manor, and in surnames as a person from a place having the suffix "-hoff."[5] Eschoff and Esch(e) are both German surnames.

There has always been the interesting rumor that Karl Friedrich may have been the illegitimate son of Friedrich der Grosse (Frederick the Great).[6] Karl Friedrich spent time at the royal court and was sent to a special school at Dessau in spite of his supposed humble origin.

To delve further into some of the most salient careers and kinship of the families Brown, Francis, Greene and Herreshoff, Nathanael Greene Herreshoff III offers the following:

Captain Nat, a seventh child, was named after Revolutionary War General Nathanael Greene of East Greenwich, Rhode Island, and his grandson Dr. Nathanael Greene of Middletown, Rhode Island. My great-grandfather, Charles Frederick Herreshoff, and Dr. Greene were close friends. Captain Nat named one of his sons Nathanael Greene Herreshoff Jr. Nat Jr. had a daughter he named Natalie. I am Nat III, my second son is Halsey II. I was recently very surprised to learn that I am a third cousin of General Greene, several generations removed. There is a great coincidence to this because I am the only Herreshoff named after a member of the Greene family who is related to them! My relationship is through my mother's family, the Chases of Prudence Island.

Captain Nat changed the spelling of his first name from Nathaniel to Nathanael late in life when he discovered the general spelled his name that way.

It is important to note that I was the first member of my direct line to graduate from college since my great-grandfather Charles Frederick Herreshoff graduated from Brown University in 1828. Neither Captain Nat nor any of his six children had college degrees. John Brown Herreshoff's granddaughters of similar age to Captain Nat's children each had two degrees.

Captain Nat's children were: Agnes Müller (1884–1965); Algernon Sidney (Sid) DeWolf (1886–1997); Nathanael Greene Jr. (1888–1926); Alexander Viets Griswold (Gid) (1889–1983); Lewis Francis (L. Francis) (1890–1972); and Clarence DeWolf (1895–1983). My grandson, Sidney Gilbert, is Captain Nat's only descendant of the latest generation. Sidney's maternal grandfather is Bristol's Reverend Fred Gilbert.

Gid Herreshoff was an automotive engineer. One of his most visible and long-lasting designs in the world of applied art is the radiator grill of the Mack Bulldog truck. While sketching ideas for the grill, he remembered Neptune's trident on the Bristol Yacht Club's pennant—the inverted trident was the inspiration for his design. Beginning around 1915, Gid began working at Chrysler Corporation, where he was highly respected as the chief engineer of development. His tenure there was for many years. In the 1930s, he had a great deal to do with the design of the streamlined Chrysler Airflow Automobile.

John Brown (J.B.) and Captain Nat's brothers James, Charles, Louis, and Julian were also very successful in their particular fields of interest.

James was a noted chemist and inventor. In the early days of the Herreshoff Manufacturing Company, he offered his expertise when he was called upon to consult on some particularly vexing problem.

Charles, as you will read in his biography further on in this book, was a farmer. He was involved in town government and had many civic and charitable interests.

Louis was blind. As an author of rank, he wrote the yachting section of the Badminton Sports Encyclopedia *of the 1890s.*

Julian, who was also blind, studied at the University of Berlin; he later founded a music school and a school of language in Providence.

J.B. and Nat's sister, Caroline's son, Albert Cheesebro (1869–1916), was a highly respected yacht designer.

John Brown Francis should not be confused with John Brown Herreshoff. J.B. the blind boat builder was named after John Brown the merchant of Providence. Francis was named after John Brown Francis—John Brown's grandson and Rhode Island governor (1833–38). The Francis family was from Dublin. John Brown's mother, Hope Power (namesake of Providence's Power Street), was also of Irish descent. Norman Herreshoff, well known in Bristol, was the grandson of John Brown Francis.

Captain Nat's first wife, Clara DeWolf, was the great-granddaughter of the Right Reverend Bishop Alexander Viets Griswold, DD (1766–1843).[7] Bishop Griswold was one of the icons in the history of the American Episcopal Church. It is also interesting to note that Clara's mother was the aunt of Father John Diman, founder of the Roman Catholic Abbey School in Portsmouth, Rhode Island. Halsey and I and Walter DeWolf are Father John's only close living relatives.

Nathanael also offered these few brief notes about the education of some of the Herreshoffs.

According to Jessie Herreshoff, who is writing a book about some of the Herreshoff women, James and John Brown Francis were brilliant students. They both graduated from Brown University. Their brother Nat was a good student, but not at the level of the other two. Nat attended MIT as a special student between 1866 and 1870, concentrating on mechanical engineering. The youngest of the brothers, Julian, who was blind, studied music and languages at the University of Berlin between 1886 and 1888. John Brown only attended Bristol schools for a while.

None of Captain Nat's children graduated from college.

Agnes graduated from Bristol High School.

Sidney attended MIT for four years studying naval architecture, French and German.

Nat Jr. and Griswold also attended MIT, but for how long I do not know.

L. Francis attended what is now URI to study agriculture.

Clarence briefly attended Brown University.

J.B.'s granddaughters were only a few years younger than Captain Nat's children. They were also double cousins. Two Herreshoffs married two DeWolfs. Katherine and Louise DeWolf both graduated from Wellesley. Katherine later earned a BS from MIT, and Louise earned her MA from BU in religious dramatics.

CHAPTER 2

NINETEENTH-CENTURY CONNECTIONS

KARL FRIEDERICH HERRESHOFF (1763–1819)

This man was an excellent linguist and a talented musician. Because of his versatile ability, he was invited to the home of John Brown almost immediately upon his arrival in the colony, beginning a friendship with the famous Rhode Island merchant that resulted not only in the entrance of the young German into the shipbuilding firm of Brown & Ives but also in his marriage (after an eleven-year courtship) to John Brown's daughter, Sarah.

According to Alicia Hopton Middleton in *Life in Carolina and New England During the Nineteenth Century*, 1929:

> *Mr. Herreshoff's grandfather was one of the bodyguards of Frederic the Great. His* [grand]*son* [Karl Frederich], *on coming to this country, was engaged in the office of John Brown of Providence and, as might be expected, a love affair soon sprang up between him and Mr. Brown's young daughter, not at all to the satisfaction of her father, she being an attractive young heiress. She was very fond of a fine horse of her father's, called Prince, and also of the old Vassall place on Pappoosesquaw* [in Bristol] *which Mr. Brown had bought, when it was confiscated at the beginning of the Revolution and Mr. Vassall expatriated on account of his sympathies with the mother country. As is generally the case in love affairs, opposition only riveted matters and finally the father succumbed to his daughter's plea that if he would give her Point Pleasant* [the Vassall property], *Prince, and Mr. Herreshoff, she would ask no more. These were granted and the "more" must have been liberally added, for the house has ever been a museum of fine old china, silver, and brocade, and its inmates from generation to generation warm and valued friends of the DeWolf household nearby.*

The son of this union, named Charles Frederick (1809–1888), eventually married Julia Ann Lewis, the daughter of a Boston sea captain, who then held the record for sailing across the Atlantic Ocean the fastest. Thus, the nine children of Charles Frederick Herreshoff and his spouse Julia Ann were born with a great percentage of maritime blood in their veins.

Being a generous father to his daughter and son-in-law, John Brown gave Karl responsibility in the management of same of the family business, at which he lost large sums of money.

In 1798, John Brown of Providence, Rhode Island, acquired 210,000 acres of land in upstate New York; this land became known as the Brown Tract. The so-called Brown Tract is located in present-day Herkimer, Lewis and Hamilton Counties. Three generations of the Brown family failed miserably in their attempts to develop the land.

In an effort to redeem himself in the eyes of the Brown family, in 1811 Karl Friederich arrived in the Browns' Adirondack Tract with his nephew, John Brown Francis. They found all of John Brown's earlier work on the roads, bridges and mills of the tract in disrepair. Herreshoff began again, but all of his ventures seemed doomed to failure. In 1815, he decided to try sheep ranching. He brought three thousand Merinoe sheep onto the land. Shortly after the sheep arrived, pillaging Algonquin destroyed the herd. The next year he wanted to establish a nail factory on the tract. The loan necessary to fund the factory was refused. This was also the "year without a summer," because of the eruption of the Tambora volcano in the Indian Ocean the previous year. This resulted in heavy snowfall in the second week of June, ruining most crops. In 1817, at staggering expense, Karl built a forge after he discovered a vane of supposed high-grade iron ore on the tract. A ton of iron was smelted, but at the exorbitant price of one dollar a pound, there was no market for it. He wrote to his daughter Anna, "There is no more doubt but that we have two sources of the most valuable ore, and both inexhaustible." Even though Herreshoff stayed on site through the winter of 1817–18 to work the mine, the ore quality was actually rather poor.

Burdened with despair, on the morning of December 19, 1819, at age fifty-six, while sitting on an outcropping of ledge on a high point overlooking his wilderness home, Karl Herreshoff sent a pistol shot crashing through his brain.

Later in 1819, Sarah, widow of John Brown, turned over the three townships she owned in the tract lands to her daughter, Abby Francis; her grandson, John Brown Francis; and her daughter, Sarah Herreshoff, Karl Friederich's widow. Abby Francis died on March 5, 1821, without heirs, at age fifty-four. Sarah Herreshoff died on August 2, 1847, at nearly seventy-three. The remainder of the Brown Tract was now in the hands of John Brown's two grandsons and namesakes: John Brown Francis and John Brown Herreshoff.

CHARLES FREDERICK HERRESHOFF JR. (1809–1888)

Charles and Julia had nine children, all of whom were born while the family lived at Point Pleasant. Among these nine were John Brown (1841–1915), Charles Frederick III (1839–1917) and Nathanael Greene (1848–1938). It was this generation of Herreshoffs that was destined to revolutionize all yacht designing and building and give to the world vessels whose like had never before been seen.

During the formative years of his youth, Charles haunted the waterfront on the town side of Bristol Harbor. There he was intrigued by the comings and goings of the hundred vessels—slavers disguised as freighters, coastal schooners and China traders; the hustle and bustle of the rough and rugged denizens of the waterfront; sailors, deckhands, coopers and crafters employed in the many tasks involved in keeping the ships rigged and afloat. This rough but friendly mix informally adopted Charles and invited him to learn, apprentice-like, their varied tasks.

Charles Frederick Jr., like his sons after him, showed at an early age a great love for the sea. At twelve he was master of a sailboat that he himself had constructed, and that he could sail with the skill of a veteran helmsman. Two years later he was known throughout the vicinity as an expert mechanic and sailor. After he graduated from Brown and returned to Bristol, he found his chief delight in building and sailing boats. Many of these were very fast and won more than a local reputation. Even after the Herreshoff Manufacturing Company had been formed, the active members of the firm received much valuable assistance and counsel from the elder Herreshoff. After his death, he was remembered as a cultured and delightful old Bristol gentleman who never spoke ill of anybody.

One amusing story relating to his boat-building career is that he always named his craft *Julia*, in honor of his wife. No amount of argument could induce him to give any of them another title. As he built successive *Julia*s, each slightly different from its predecessor, he would give the earlier craft to one of his children. Mrs. Herreshoff occupied the homestead on Hope Street, opposite the shops of the company, until her death.

In his book *The Boatbuilders of Bristol*, Samuel Carter III writes several amusing antidotes about life at Point Pleasant Farm. One story is about the plethora of inventions being thought up or in use at the farm. Charles made a revolving iron stove, which permitted Julia to spin cooking pots from one burner to another by the touch of a finger. He also contrived a mechanical lawn mower to spare himself the backache of swinging a scythe.

Creative thinking among Charles and his sons never ceased. Reasoning that if wind can drive a ship across the ocean it could certainly drive other things, windmills sprouted around Point Pleasant like mushrooms. Indeed, when observing a boiling pot's top blown off by the force of the steam, Charles reasoned that steam in a controlled environment could be energy converted to motive power.

We learn some interesting history about the Herreshoff family's connection to Portsmouth, Rhode Island's Prudence Island from Joseph J. Bains's privately published 1997 book, *The Prudence Inn Land from Prudence Farm to Prudence Conservancy*:

> *Land on Prudence Island that had been acquired by John Brown, which totaled 1,570 acres, later passed to his son, James Brown (1761–1834). When James died, much of this land including Baker Farm passed to his sister Sarah (1773–1846), the widow of Karl Friedrich Herreshoff (1763–1819).*
>
> *When Sarah died, she willed her three farms on Prudence Island (approximately 1,200 acres), to her five* [surviving] *children* [which included Charles Frederick].

CHARLES FREDERICK HERRESHOFF III (1839–1917)

Charles was the last of the Herreshoffs to vacate the Point Pleasant homestead. His brothers and sisters, aunts and uncles had homes on the town side of Bristol Harbor. The old Vassall house, by then well over a century old, sadly, had fallen into decay. Thus, Charles was prompted to build a house on another section of the land. Here he settled down as a ruddy-cheeked gentleman farmer cultivating beets and the hardy Bristol onion. Poultry too was in bountiful supply on Charles and Alice's farm. Alice delivered vegetables and chickens by boat to town shops. This income supplemented the allowance given by his brother John.

It should be noted that this Herreshoff man was not the least lacking in creativity; he had his share of the family's ability to come up with novel ideas. As a tribute to his ailing back, he invented his ambulatory stool, which allowed him to weed his garden while seated rather than trudging along from plant to plant and row to row on his knees. He is alleged to be the first poultry farmer in New England to heat his chicken houses with central heating.

Charles Frederick was a lover of fine whiskey and tobacco; it is said he was seldom invited to gatherings of cultured society because he would indiscriminately squirt tobacco juice on fine floor coverings and furniture. Even though he was ostracized from polite society, he did gain a seat on the Bristol Town Council, and at one time served as the council's president.

Charles Frederick died of natural causes, on his beloved farm, in early 1917 at age seventy-eight.

THE HERRESHOFF FAMILY IN THE 1880S

This family history is offered by Nathanael G. Herreshoff III.

> *Two focal points in the history of the Herreshoff family in the nineteenth century are the fiftieth wedding anniversary party for Charles Frederick and Julia Ann Lewis Herreshoff in 1883, and the photograph of their family on the front porch at 140 Hope Street the following year. Charles and Julia were married by the reverend Motte in Boston on May 15, 1833. They made their home soon afterward at Point Pleasant Farm on Poppasquash Point facing the harbor in Bristol, Rhode Island. Nine children were born to them between 1834 and 1854.*
>
> *In 1856, the family moved across the harbor to town at 142 Hope Street. Several of Charles's relatives remained at Point Pleasant Farm. At first the Herreshoffs rented the house until 1863, when Julia bought it with a mortgage. Thereafter the house was moved back from the road and an addition made in the rear. Also in 1863, John Brown Herreshoff began his boat building business nearby.*
>
> *Next door to the south of 142 Hope Street a house was built probably in 1878. This house has been called the Herreshoff Manufacturing Company Guest House, where guests*

and clients of the company were lodged. Mrs. Caroline Chesebrough (sometimes spelled Chesebro) lived there with her son, Albert. Her husband, Ebenezer Stanton Chesebrough, originally from New York State, died in 1875.

Living at 140 Hope Street were Caroline Chesebrough, age forty-three; her son Albert, age twelve; and a domestic from Ireland, Mary McLaughlin, age twenty-eight.

The golden wedding anniversary party was held on Tuesday, May 15, 1883, between two and five o'clock at Mrs. Chesebrough's residence. The sons and daughters of Charles and Julia hosted the party. Their eldest son, James, and his family were not present because they were still in Europe. More than one hundred invitations were sent out and a large crowd was present.

Much of what we know of the party is taken from an article in the Bristol Phoenix. It is said that many prominent persons, including a large number from Providence and elsewhere, were present. It was also noted that a large number of ladies were there. Mrs. Chesebrough's residence was decked out in floral emblems. Many bouquets were also received from friends of the family. There were numerous presents consisting of many elegant ornamental and useful articles. Among the gifts were fine gold watches and chains given to each parent by their nine children. According to the article, "Mr. and Mrs. Herreshoff received all with that pleasant, graceful and dignified manner, which characterizes the true gentleman and lady. Refreshments were served in abundance."

The Herreshoff family home at 142 Hope Street, circa 1902, photo by K. Herreshoff DeWolf. *Courtesy Herreshoff Marine Museum.*

The famous picture of the Herreshoff family taken on the 142 Hope Street porch was probably taken in 1884.[8] The census of 1880 reveals much about the Herreshoff family at that time. To the north of 142 Hope Street lived Julian Herreshoff, youngest son of Charles and Julia, his wife Ellen and her brother, Walter E. Taft. A machinist also lived there as a boarder. There was also one domestic, Clara Frieda, from Saxony in Germany. At 142 Hope Street there were a large number of official residents; they are listed as follows:

Name	Relationship	Age	Birthplace	Remarks
Charles F. Herreshoff	Husband	70	Rhode Island	Retired farmer
Julia A. Herreshoff	Wife	69	Massachusetts	
James B. Herreshoff	Son	46	Rhode Island	Chemist, traveling in Europe
Jane B. Herreshoff	Daughter-in-law	24	Ireland	Traveling in Europe
Jane B. Herreshoff	Granddaughter	3	New York	Traveling in Europe
James B. Herreshoff Jr.	Grandson	2	England	Traveling in Europe
Lewis Herreshoff	Son	36	Rhode Island	Blind
Nathanael G. Herreshoff	Son	32	Rhode Island	Mechanical engineer
Mary W. Lewis	Sister-in-law	63	Massachusetts	Divorced
Louise E. Brown	Domestic	13	Prussia	
Emma M. Friede	Domestic	16	Prussia	
Joanna O'Brien	Domestic	16	Ireland	

CHAPTER 3

JOHN BROWN HERRESHOFF
(1841–1915)

The story of the Herreshoff Manufacturing Company must start with John Brown Herreshoff. At the time of his birth, the Herreshoffs were living at Point Pleasant Farm on Poppasquash Neck. He showed a great deal of energy and ambition for a lad, having his own rope walk, a workshop and a foot lathe. He had a natural and dominant interest in boats; it was in his blood.

Known locally as J.B., John Brown Herreshoff was a most remarkable man who, in spite of being blind for most of his life, started and ran a thriving boat building business in Bristol for fifty-two years. Known in history as "the blind designer" and "the blind boat builder," he was a person of great ambition and ability along with a quick mind who developed his nonvisual senses to a high degree to overcome the handicap of sightlessness.

At age seven, John Brown was deprived of sight in one eye because of an illness; later, he lost the sight in his other eye from an accident while playing with his brother Charles.

J.B. was seven years older than his brother Nat; he was an aggressive and impatient taskmaster to his younger brother, who was forced to do things far beyond what would normally be expected of a boy his age. While these activities may have been interesting, they were no doubt a burden and probably deprived the young lad of a normal childhood. This had a marked effect on Nat's character.

In 1856, the entire family moved from Point Pleasant Farm across the harbor, to a house that stands at 142 Hope Street just south of Burnside Street. Two years later J.B. began his boat building business.

Thus, when J.B., totally without sight at the age of eighteen, accepted a commission to design and build a yacht for Thomas Clapham, he began an industry that thrived beyond all expectations and brought international fame and honor to himself and to Bristol, Rhode Island. In his early years, Herreshoff had acquired such a keen knowledge and "feel" of boats that his blindness was no obstacle. The handwork, however, was done by his brother, Nathanael Greene Herreshoff, later known as "the Wizard of Bristol."

John Brown Herreshoff had an exceptional memory and a photographic mind. His method was to dictate specifications to his brother, who would construct a model. Then, by feeling the model, J.B. could find defects and suggest improvements with uncanny intuition.

John Brown Herreshoff. *Courtesy* Leslie's Illustrated Newspaper.

At the beginning of his work in 1863, John—then only twenty-two years old—hired a crew of men, procured supplies of seasoned lumber and fitted out an old tannery as a shop. In the following year, nine sailing craft, ranging in length from twenty-two to thirty-five feet, were launched. As the business grew, an additional building on Burnside Street—the old Ambrose E. Burnside Rifle Factory—was bought and converted to a sawmill for producing the enterprise's lumber. In 1864, J.B. formed a temporary partnership with Dexter Stone that lasted four years.

By 1868, Herreshoff Manufacturing had built its first steamer, the *Annie Morse*, followed in 1870 by the *Seven Brothers*, a pioneer fishing steamer on the Atlantic Coast that was built for the Church brothers of Tiverton, Rhode Island.

There is more to the creation of a quality yacht than vision and genius in design. The Herreshoff Manufacturing Company took yachts from the drawing board to the water with a quality of workmanship that was unsurpassed. Despite his blindness, John Brown Herreshoff was able to build and run a successful boat building business. He had a great capacity for business, and with his younger brother Nat taking over the design work for the company and supervision of the technical aspects concerned with construction, J.B. became completely free to run the business end, at which he excelled. He did the job costing for their boats, an extremely challenging job under any circumstances but an absolutely amazing feat and testament to his genius, considering that he did all the math in his head. He was the one to negotiate and close the deals for new boat orders and was also a good manager, keeping up the enthusiasm of his employees.

Under the new partnership, the business soared from twenty or thirty employees to over four hundred employees. The men worked very efficiently under a strict but fair set of rules. As far as is known, labor relations were always excellent and "Mr. John" and

Engine crew. *Left to right, front row*: Foreman Ben Wood, (?) Wilson, Bob Cook, C. "Charley Cooper" Ruprecat, Tom Brightman Sr.; *back row*: Jim "Chief" Robertson, Jimmy Wood, Harry Monroe, unknown, Sam Monroe, unknown. *Courtesy Herreshoff Marine Museum.*

"Mr. Nat" were generally well liked and respected. All work was always of the highest quality and was envied throughout the boating industry.

On his inspection tours of the yard, J.B. used a special cane and watch with which he could make all kinds of measurements to determine lengths, diameters and so on with remarkable ease. He possessed an incredible ability to do mental mathematics; he would sit for a while and figure out the cost of a new yacht, which involved all kinds of material, and labor costs with amazing accuracy. He had an exceptional ability to calculate the potential speed of a boat by passing his hand over a model; he could tell more about its value than most men who had use of their eyes.

One story of his surprising ability to carry accounts in his head related to his experience with representatives of the government of Peru who wished to contract for three American-built SPAR torpedo boats. The South Americans described their needs to J.B. and asked him his price for construction.

"I shall require some time to consider the matter," he responded, as the craft were of a novel pattern and possessed some features that made the task of calculating their cost especially difficult.

Machine shop crew, circa 1914. *Left to right, front row*: Harry Seymour, Ned Lindsey, Tom Morey, Dave Walker, Charlie Brigham (foreman), Armand deConig, Herbert "Bugger" Lord, (?) Sellers, Walter Handy; *back row*: Clarence Seymour, Harold June, Charley Weaver, Dick Hibbert and Mr. Cole. *Courtesy Herreshoff Marine Museum.*

"But how much time?" he was asked.

"Half an hour," was his reply. At the expiration of that interval, J.B. presented figures that were so satisfactory to the men that they immediately ordered the boats.

In October 1870, J.B. married Sarah Kilton of Boston. They had one daughter, Katherine, known to the family as Katie, who was born in 1871. Katie and her father were always very close and she accompanied him often in Bristol and on his travels abroad. In April 1892, after a California divorce from Sarah Kilton, J.B. married Eugenia Tams Tucker of Bristol.

For many years J.B. lived on Burnside Street in the midst of the yard. Later, he built a large Second Empire–style house that still sits on High Street at the head of Burnside Street. He also owned many rental properties in Bristol, and around 1900 he built the Belvedere Hotel on Hope Street in the center of the bustling business district for the convenience of wealthy clients who came to town to watch the construction and take delivery of their yachts. During slack times at the yard, workmen were often involved in house building and renovation. Visitors who cast their eyes upon houses on High and Hope Streets and numerous side streets will notice ceilings of piazza roofs with structural supports shaped like the ribs of a boat.

In later years, J.B.'s personal boating activities were largely confined to steam yachts. He built several to which he gave his wife's name, Eugenia. It is of interest to note that several works of popular fiction have references to their characters owning or ordering boats from "the Herreshoff Brothers."

J.B.'s personal yacht, the *Eugenia*, is seen in Bristol Harbor with the Naval Reserve Armory in the background, circa 1899. This impressive boat—LOA ninety-five feet, beam fourteen feet, draft nine feet six inches—was a steel flush deck yacht powered by quadruple-expansion engine with bent tub boiler and thirty-six-inch screw. *Courtesy Herreshoff Marine Museum.*

During the 1880s, the yard continued to build mostly steam vessels, including the speedy *Stiletto*, which won the celebrated 1885 race on the Hudson River against the so-called Queen of the Hudson, the *Mary Powell*. Beginning in the 1890s the yard shifted away from steamers to the production of sailing yachts.

In the spring of 1915, Captain Nat returned to Bristol after having spent the winter in Bermuda. He and J.B. had an argument behind closed doors concerning the building of torpedo boats for the Russian navy. Nat was suspicious about the deal and advised against it. Nat reminded his brother and partner of their agreement never to do business unless reserved funds were on hand. After the conference, J.B. walked home and never returned to the yard. The contract was not concluded. John Brown Herreshoff died shortly after, on July 20, 1915, at the age of seventy-four.

DEXTER SHELDON STONE: PARTNER OF JOHN BROWN HERRESHOFF (1864–1867)

Nathanael G. Herreshoff III also provided the following information on J.B.'s business partner.

> *Dexter Sheldon Stone was born on December 1, 1837, in Coventry, Rhode Island. He was the second of five children born to Dexter Greene Stone (1812–1887) and Elizabeth Lillibridge Stone. An ancestor, Hugh Stone, was in Rhode Island as early as the 1650s. Dexter Greene Stone was listed in the Providence City directory of 1862 as running a stable and living at 7 Federal Street.*
>
> *Dexter Sheldon Stone was educated in Providence at the Summer Street Grammar School and the Providence High School. He attended Brown University, graduating in 1857 with a PhD, and was listed by the university as a civil engineer. In 1862 he was listed in the city directory as a book agent and living at 7 Federal Street.*
>
> *John Brown Herreshoff established his boat building business in 1863. In 1864, J.B. formed a partnership with Dexter Sheldon Stone. The business was known as Herreshoff and Stone and lasted until 1867, when it was dissolved. What the terms of the partnership were are not known at the present time. According to John's brother, Nat, in a letter written in 1937, Dexter did all the correspondence and accounting, but differences soon came up and the partnership ended.*
>
> *Before going into partnership with J.B., Dexter had sailed and cruised with the Herreshoffs in their sailboat the* Kelpie. *In 1866 J.B. and Dexter were elected as founding members of the Boston Yacht Club at its first meeting.*
>
> *In the genealogy of the Stone family written in 1866 by Richard C. Stone, Dexter is described as "a young man with much energy of character and fine promise." After leaving his partnership with J.B. he joined the large publishing house of Coperthwaite & Co. of Philadelphia, eventually became a partner and remained there for the rest of his life. He assisted Professor Dana Colburn in editing his mental arithmetic and Professor Greene in compiling his English grammar. Dexter was one of the compilers of* Warren's Geography *and other schoolbooks,*

especially readers. He managed the firm's educational department for many years up to the time of his death.

Dexter was married to Amelia B. Brockett and had one child named Edith.

Suffering from stomach cancer in 1887, Dexter came to Nantucket for six weeks, where he died on August 8. He was cited in his Providence Journal *obituary as "a great lover of the water and passionately fond of yachting." He is buried in New Haven, Connecticut.*

CHAPTER 4

NATHANAEL GREENE HERRESHOFF (1848–1938)

Doctor Nathanael Greene, son of the American Revolutionary War general from East Greenwich, Rhode Island, often visited the Herreshoff family at Point Pleasant Farm. Doctor Greene was a classmate of Charles Frederick Jr.'s at Brown University at Providence. He took a special interest in his and his father's namesake, the boy who would become Captain Nat, "the Wizard of Bristol." Doctor Greene gave the young Nathanael a jackknife, "made in England for New England whalers."

In 1859, at the age of eleven, Nathanael Greene Herreshoff had the job of taking sections from half models for drawings and scaling them for laying down the lines for construction at his older brother's boat shop. At this tender age, Nat built the *Sprite* so that he and his brother could sail to New York City to view the *Great Eastern*.[9] Nat also served as helmsman for J.B. They were quite successful in racing. J.B. had a remarkable sense of wind direction and for the feel of a boat underway.

Nat became an impatient perfectionist as well as an innovator and experimenter. Throughout his lifetime, the relationship between him and J.B. was rather complicated

He was a naval architect-engineer. He revolutionized yacht design and produced a succession of undefeated sailboats for the 1893–1920 America's Cup races, now referred to as the "Herreshoff Period." The yachts he designed were the largest, most expensive and most powerful ever created to defend yachting's supreme prize.

Nat attended the Massachusetts Institution of Technology in 1870, where he studied mechanical engineering. He later took a position with the Corliss Steam Engine Company in Providence. At the 1876 Philadelphia Centennial Exposition, he oversaw operation of the Corliss Stationary Engine, a forty-foot-tall, 1,400-horsepower dynamo that supplied the energy to power the exhibition's thirteen acres of machinery.

Tragedy struck in 1888, when Nat was supervising speed trials of a 138-foot, 875-horsepower steamer, the *Say When*. A safety valve popped, and he screwed it down to allow the boat to achieve its anticipated speed. Suddenly, a tube in the boiler exploded, fatally injuring a member of the crew. Consequently, Nat lost his steam engineer's license.

Though the Herreshoff Manufacturing Company created the U.S. Navy's first torpedo boats, as well as launches and powerboats, the company is best remembered for their sailing boats and yachts of exceeding grace.

Nathanael Greene Herreshoff. *Courtesy* Leslie's Illustrated Newspaper.

In the 1890s Nathanael, by then known as Captain Nat, favored designing sailing yachts. He hit upon the innovative timesaving idea of building hulls upside down, with a mold for every frame, and of the lightest possible materials aloft. The firm supplied vessels to the elite of its day, including Jay Gould, William Randolph Hearst, J.P. Morgan, Cornelius Vanderbilt, Harold S. Vanderbilt, William K. Vanderbilt, Harry Payne Whitney and others.

Captain Nat designed and built a wide range of craft, including the Doughdish, also known as the Bullseye class (originally called the Buzzards Bay Boys Boat), a small sailboat used to train children of yachtsmen. He was also responsible for the *New York 30* class ("30" refers to waterline length) and the 143-foot America's Cup behemoth *Reliance*, with a sail area of 17,000 square feet. The 123-foot *Defender* was equally astounding, due to its radical construction; it featured steel framing, bronze plating up to the waterline and aluminum topsides. As might be expected, when placed in the ocean's saline, the boat's galvanic corrosion was immediate. It won the race, and then began dissolving.

Most designs by the Wizard of Bristol have fared better, and today they are highly prized by connoisseurs of classic yachts. The site of the Herreshoff Manufacturing Company is now a museum dedicated to the preservation of the Herreshoff yachting legacy.

Nathanael Greene Herreshoff is acknowledged as one of the greatest yacht and marine designers and builders that America has ever produced. He brought grace, beauty and speed to yachting and is credited with the introduction of more new devices in the design of boats than any other man. Literally, he was to yachting what Einstein was to science and what Picasso was to art.

During his seventy-two-year career Captain Nat designed and built five winning America's Cup yachts: the *Vigilant* in 1893; the *Defender* in 1895; the *Columbia*, built for the 1899 competition, raced again in 1901; the *Reliance*, built in 1903; and the *Resolute*, built in 1914, won the Cup in 1920. He sailed them as well, earning a reputation as a most proficient and skilled helmsman. Additionally, the Herreshoff Manufacturing Company built two winning Cup yachts designed by Starling Burgess: the *Enterprise* in 1930 and the *Rainbow* in 1934. In short, every winning America's Cup yacht from 1893 to 1934 was built by Herreshoff!

It is an almost unbelievable accomplishment that Nat designed well over two thousand craft and produced more than eighteen thousand drawings. Between 1890 and 1938, yachts he designed won the Astor Cup, Puritan Cup and Kings Cup. His winning yachts outnumbered the combined wins by all the other yacht designers.

Captain Nat, a quiet man, never boasted of his accomplishments. It is we, his admirers, who must number his record of successes; in the world of sail racing his knowledge and advancements for the sport include his calculation of the original table for giving the minutes and seconds that a larger yacht must allow a smaller one, making it possible for yachts of different size to race together. He also designed the Universal Rule for the New York Yacht Club, which became the accepted standard in yachting.

His marine inventions include the streamline-shaped bulb and fin keels; the sail track and slide in its present form along with many other patterns of marine hardware; and the overhangs on sailing yachts to allow longer lines and greater stability. It is well known among maritime historians that he developed the first light steam engine and fast torpedo boats; he designed and the Herreshoff Manufacturing Company built the first all-steel, sea-going torpedo boats for the United States Navy.

The innovative Captain Nat developed nearly all of the methods of constructing lightweight wooden hulls; he introduced screw fastenings for planking in America; he invented the crosscut sail with cloths running at right angles to the leech.

Yachts in winter storage, at nearby Walker's Cove.

It is astounding to note that Captain Nat is the designer of more types of steam engines than anyone else. He designed the web frame and longitudinal construction for metal hulls, afterward patented and known as the Isherwood System. He also developed the light hollow steel spars combined with scientific rigging. It was Captain Nat who first developed the flat stern form of steam yachts capable of being driven at high speed/ length ratios; his innovative folding propeller allowed his steam yachts to obtain record speeds for the era.

The Wizard of Bristol cannot be denied credit for his conception and installation of below-deck winches (as on *Reliance*, 1903) and his original method of splicing rope to wire. To his everlasting credit, he owns the first U.S. patent on catamaran sailboats, from 1877.

Because of his many accomplishments, he was one of the few people ever to have been made an honorary life member of the New York Yacht Club, his name being listed immediately before His Majesty King George V and the Prince of Wales.

His fame spread around the world and the period of his greatest activity from 1890 to 1920 became known as the "Herreshoff Era," so greatly did his personality and the yachts he designed dominate the sport. It is undisputed that Nat Herreshoff was a genius and a master, which earned him the nickname the Wizard of Bristol.

CAPTAIN NAT'S PERSONA

During conversations with Nathanael Greene Herreshoff III, we discussed several bits of hearsay published by various writers about Captain Nat's personality. He said, "I would be very careful in writing about Captain Nat's personality. Much of what has been written is simply not right. My late cousin Natalie agreed with me about this. I may be the only person still around who knew him well. He lived next door to me until he died when I was seven years old."

Nathanael Greene continued with his personal recollections of the strengths and sensitivities of his grandfather. He said,

> *Captain Nat was a man of principle. My grandfather was a very kindly and moral man; he was also very determined and focused. Determined and focused; he was of course very organized in whatever he did.*
>
> *Although the Herreshoffs of Bristol have been devout Episcopalians, as far as I know, Captain Nat did not have much to do with formal religion. But I do believe he was a person of definite ideas and beliefs.*
>
> *Among his closest friends was Frank H. Brown of the Warwick, Rhode Island branch of relatives, and Commodore Monroe of the Miami area. He was very friendly with the famous yachtsman E.D. Morgan. It was this friendship with Morgan that had much to do with the design of the* Gloriana *and the* Wasp. *Of course, he and Captain Charlie Barr had much respect for each other and they worked well together.*
>
> *The family subscribed to the* Herald Tribune *for weekdays and the* New York Times *on Sunday—because the* Times *had better yachting coverage. The* Times *has always been my best research source when writing yachting history.*
>
> *One particular story relates Nat's commitment to his belief in his yacht designs. A customer of distinction ordered a new design from the yard after his boat was soundly defeated in a regatta. Nat sent a sketch for a boat with a deeper keel, to which the customer replied it was unacceptable because the water in the harbor was too shallow to accommodate it. Nat replied, "Recommend dredging." The customer was German Kaiser Wilhelm II.*

Nat was a man of restrained character, not prone to jocular or angry outbursts. It appeared he liked his own company better than the association of many friends because his head was evidently full of new ideas. Judging by the number of new ideas he evolved and published to the world, he did not have to depend on anybody but himself for entertainment. In the course of his years of work in Bristol, he must have been "thinking up" something new during most of his waking moments. He walked along the town's streets with his head inclined forward, as if he were in search of some novel notion. There was a local tale that he acquired the habit from watching his rivals in his races, craning his head in order to see them from under the boom.

Captain Nat's large, comfortable home at Bristol, built as sturdy as one of his yachts, is called Love Rocks. It still stands facing west into Bristol Harbor. The house is constructed on an outcrop of ledge near the end of Hope Street, with its back to the street; it is not far from the boatyard. The house's isolation and the fact that it fronts Bristol Harbor are indicative of the attitude of its owner toward the general public. The unspoken command, "Do not disturb," was understood. His chief inspiration always

Captain Nat's residence on Bristol Harbor. Called Love Rocks, the house takes its name from the outcropping of ledge on the left. In the left background can be seen the south boat shop, circa 1937. *Courtesy Herreshoff Marine Museum.*

came from the sea. His windows look far down Narragansett Bay, with Poppasquash Point stretching to the south and Prudence Island in the foreground. It is a picturesque bit of scenery, and as Captain Nat had an interesting family it is no wonder that he was satisfied with his home.

A certain Captain Albert C. Bennett, a Bristol veteran of sixty-four ocean crossings in sailing vessels, sailed with the Herreshoffs, both father and son, a greater number of times, probably, than any other one man. Captain Bennett said he only saw Nat excited in a race once. It was in a race in Gowanus Bay, when the future designer of America's Cup defenders was at the helm. The breeze slackened, and it was thought advisable to raise a topsail, but in the course of this operation one of the corners got away from the crew and the sail went flapping high into the air. Captain Nat took off his cap, flung it down on the deck and the language in which he indulged himself for a moment is said to have been extremely "forcible."

"But that's the only time," said Captain Bennett, "that I ever saw him when he seemed to be excited." As the yachting fraternity knows very well, Nat was uniformly cool and careful in a race, sailing his craft for "all she is worth," making few tactical errors.

On one occasion he was steering the *Janthe* in a race in the vicinity of New York when the breeze almost deserted the boats and left them idly moving in the direction of home, but at a snail's pace. There were two or more classes of yachts in the fleet, but the skipper

Captain Nat always kept his favorite boats at the ready at the Love Rocks dock, circa 1913.
Courtesy Herreshoff Marine Museum.

of the *Janthe*, steering wide of his comrades, ran into a little breeze he had seen far to
starboard, and beat all the classes over the finish line. It was by such careful and cool-
headed observation that opens possibilities to the wide-awake helmsman in every race
that he won his great reputation as a sailor.

CAPTAIN NAT'S SUSPICION OF SPIES

Nat Herreshoff was known to be secretive and taciturn to the point of paranoia. The
following paragraphs accurately summarize one aspect of the personality of the most
brilliant naval architect the America's Cup has ever known.

For his entire life, Nat was haunted by a fear of having his ideas stolen, of being
victimized by a spy. He posted armed guards at the boat sheds where his successful
defenders were being built, in an effort to push away the curious and discourage
intrusive photographers. His attitude is commonplace today: a quick walk around the
Port America's Cup in Valencia, Spain—where the 2007 Cup races are scheduled to play
out—will verify that. But for his time, it was extremely unusual and obsessive behavior.

Herreshoff focused on his profession as an exclusive passion, to the detriment of his
close relations. After the death in 1891 of his friend Edward Burgess, who had designed
three victorious defenders (*Puritan* in 1885, *Mayflower* in 1886 and *Volunteer* in 1887),

Captain Nat used to welcome Burgess's son, William Starling, to Bristol for the holidays. The teenager spent hours watching his "Uncle" Nat carve his models.

Near the end of 1896, the young Burgess followed the construction of the *Sally II*, a small five-meter boat that had been conceived by Herreshoff as an eighteenth birthday gift for him. During its construction, the teenager confided his ambition to become a naval architect, like his father. Nat's reaction was swift and harsh; he expelled Burgess from his workshop, banishing him from seeing any of his work in progress. This didn't prevent Burgess from realizing his goal to become a designer. In fact, he would design Cup defenders three times between 1930 and 1937, including the J-class boats *Enterprise*, *Rainbow* and the *Ranger*, designed with Olin Stephens.

The Wizard of Bristol wasn't discriminatory in his paranoia. He had the same reaction to his own son, L. Francis, who was also very interested in his father's work. Aggravated, Nat sent his son to the Rhode Island State Agricultural School, which today is the University of Rhode Island. L. Francis settled into his work as a farmer before becoming a renowned designer who created the unsuccessful defense candidate, the J-class *Whirlwind*, in the 1930 competition for the Cup.

Captain Nat had a fear of spies for his entire working life and lived in constant suspicion of people stealing his ideas. He did, however, inspire an entire generation of designers. Although he was not a victim of any obvious act of espionage, his paranoia also inspired the secrecy that hovers over the Cup to this day.

CAPTAIN NAT'S CATAMARANS

Nat was twenty-nine in 1877, when he brought out his famous catamarans. While on leave from Corliss, he began building commercially available catamarans. Cats were well known in the Pacific, but were new in this country; he made use of a novel idea by joining the two canoe-like hulls of which these exotic craft are composed, thus revolutionizing their construction. He entered his catamaran, the *Amaryllis*, in a New York Yacht Club race, sailing past all in sight, for which the New York Yacht Club promptly rewarded him by banning multihulls from racing!

In *Herreshoff of Bristol*, authors Maynard Bray and Carlton Pinheiro offer the following paragraphs concerning Nat's commercial line of cats:

> *Nat produced seven catamarans, starting in 1875 with* Amaryllis, *built by J.B.'s boatyard crew. Two years later, after patenting his design, he went into business for himself, offering catamarans in three sizes: a 20-footer for three to four persons, a 25-footer for five to six persons, and a 32-footer for seven or eight, "these to be furnished complete with anchors and cables, storm jibs, built of the best material, and guaranteed." The endeavor proved unsuccessful, and only three more catamarans were built under this arrangement. Their cost was higher than anticipated, and, after a brief return to the Corliss Steam Engine Co., in the fall of 1877, Nat joined his brother to form the Herreshoff Mfg. Co.*

The catamaran called *Amaryllis*, built about 1877 to Captain Nat's patent. *Courtesy Herreshoff Marine Museum.*

Nat was quoted in the *Eastern Yacht Club Ditty Box* as saying he conceived the idea of constructing a double-hulled sailboat, by which great stability could be obtained with little weight and easy lines. Nat's cats sailed very fast, and would make twenty miles per hour on a close reach and eight miles per hour dead to windward. He said he enjoyed sailing these craft more than any other he had owned.

Before Nat's innovative hull connection, catamarans consisted of two hulls united by an unjointed series of braces; but he introduced a flexible joint, by means of which the hulls acted almost independently of each other. They accommodated themselves to the waves in much better fashion, and the result was that Nat beat nearly every craft he encountered.

It is told that one day Nat lay in wait off the mouth of Bristol Harbor for the steamer from Newport. When she came abreast, with the wind blowing briskly up the bay, he headed his strange-looking craft in the same direction, and beat the steamer to Providence so badly that the fame of his boat spread far and wide.

It is also said that Nat made twenty-one miles in an hour over a measured course in one of his catamarans. On another occasion, in a yacht race off Sandy Hook, he tarried

Captain Nat's catamaran, the *Lodoala*, sporting a boom tent making cruising possible, circa 1877. *Courtesy Herreshoff Marine Museum.*

about the starting line with his double-hulled craft until all the contestants had gotten far down the course. One of the crew onboard another boat said he and others watched the queer craft putting out long after they had set off on the race, and followed its progress with interest. Nearer and nearer came Nat, and before long he had passed not only this particular boat but also every yacht in the fleet. This was one of Nat's quiet little jokes.

WILL OF N.G. HERRESHOFF
The will of Nathanael Greene Herreshoff, who died on June 2, 1938, was filed in the Bristol Probate Court on June 9, 1938.

Captain Nat's 1877 patent model for his flexible pontoon catamaran. *Courtesy Herreshoff Marine Museum.*

To his daughter, Agnes Herreshoff, are bequeathed the set of china once owned by John Brown, a loving cup presented to him in 1899 by his employees, a set of Life and Works of the Sisters Bronte, and an old four inch telescope given him by William Young.

To his son Sidney Herreshoff is to go a gold cup given him by John DeWolf, a model measuring instrument with a pantograph attachment and a K&E Amster Planimeter.

To his son, Griswold Herreshoff, is to go a gold watch and chain given him by his brother John in 1881, said watch having an Elgin movement and an engraving of a catamaran and a monogram on the case, "these engravings being valued by me as being designed by my old friend, George Gould Philips," and a silver tankard presented to him by Commodore Morgan "as a souvenir of Gloriana's victories in 1891."

His son, Francis, is to receive a set of books entitled, "Society of Naval Architects and Marine Engineers" [and] "the old and much valued double-barreled shot gun that was formerly the prized fowling-piece of Dr. Nathanael Greene, of Newport, a Ballard rifle and Winchester repeating shotgun."

To his son, Clarence, Mr. Herreshoff bequeaths his Alvin Clark telescope, "the three great volumes of Naval Architecture of John Scott-Russel, these volumes being now rare and valuable," a gold watch presented by Commodore Robert E. Tod in 1914 at the launching of the schooner yacht "Katoura."

To his wife is bequeathed a collection of china left him by his brother-in-law, John DeWolf, and a silver cup presented by the Managers of the yacht "Resolute." All other household furnishings, china, silver, etc., not noted to thoroughly furnish "Love Rocks" homestead are to be divided among his wife, children and grandchildren.

Nathanael Chase Herreshoff, his grandson, is to receive his fourth model-yacht named "Sprite," which Mr. Herreshoff made, when the boy is eleven years old, or prior to that time if he has made a successful toy sailing boat and, hence, has so become somewhat familiar with the use of tools.

The undivided one-eighth interest which he has in Point Pleasant Farm on Poppasquash Neck in Bristol is bequeathed to his son, Lewis Francis Herreshoff.

All the rest, residue and remainder of the estate is to be held in trust with the Rhode Island Hospital Trust Company as Trustee. By the terms of the trust, his wife, Ann Roebuck Herreshoff, is to be allowed to occupy the homestead free of rent during her lifetime, as is also his daughter, Agnes.

The net income from the trust estate is to be paid in varying proportions to his wife, children and two grandchildren, children of his deceased son, Nathanael. In case his wife and daughter shall cease to occupy the homestead then it becomes a part of the general trust fund. Upon such change of status, the Trustee is authorized to lease the estate at a minimum rental to such of his children "in order of preference according to their age" as desire to occupy it.

Income from the trust estate is also to be paid annually as follows: Benjamin Church Home, Bristol, $75; Bristol Home for Aged Women, $75; Bristol Children's Home, $75; Bristol District Nursing Association, $75; Rhode Island Hospital, $100.

Three years after the decease of his wife, the trust estate is to be divided among the children.

The Rhode Island Trust Company is named as Executor.

CHAPTER 5
TWENTIETH-CENTURY CONNECTIONS

JAMES BROWN HERRESHOFF (1834–1930)

During his long life, James Brown's accomplishments were legend. This member of Bristol's inventive Herreshoff family was no less an innovative thinker than his brothers, cousins and uncles. With his brother, Captain Nat, James helped perfect the coil-steam boiler and the fin keel used on sailing yachts.

James was born in Bristol on Point Pleasant Farm in 1834 to Charles Frederick and Julia Ann Louis. He studied at Brown University from 1853 to 1856, and at age forty-one he married Jane Brown of Dromore, Ireland. The couple had five children, and in keeping with the family's tradition of passing family names to succeeding generations, the children were christened James Brown Jr., Charles Frederick, William Stuart, Jane Brown and Anna Francis Herreshoff.

James was a talented chemist and from 1852 to 1863 he was employed by the Rumford Chemical Works in East Providence, Rhode Island. Possibly one of his most innovative triumphs was his invention and construction of the first internal combustion naphtha-powered motorcycle in America. He often collaborated with his brothers, J.B. and Captain Nat, and gave creative insight to particularly sticky technical problems that occurred in the development of the coil boiler.

After 1869, and for several years, James spent a great deal of his time abroad representing his brothers' Bristol boatyard. It was he, along with enthusiastic European owners of Herreshoff yachts, who acted as sales agent for the Bristol product. We must assume that all his time in Europe was not entirely applied to business interests, because James was a patron of the arts and spent much of his time collecting.

Although J.B. and Captain Nat were responsible for the design of the company's Cup defenders, luxury yachts and speedy steamers, James Brown can rightfully be credited for many improvements and advancements in designs embodied in these boats.

Among James's inventions were mercurial anti-fouling paint, a sliding seat for rowboats, the thread tension regulator for sewing machines and an apparatus for measuring the specific heat of gasses.

James Brown Herreshoff died at age ninety-six at his home in Riverdale, New York. He is buried in Bristol.

LEWIS FRANCIS HERRESHOFF (1890–1972)

L. Francis Herreshoff was born in Bristol, Rhode Island, near the waters of Narragansett Bay, an area long noted for its yachting activity. His father, Nathanael Greene Herreshoff, was one of the most prominent yacht designers and manufacturers of boats in the world. L. Francis developed his father's skills at an early age, later becoming equally recognized as a respected and influential designer and builder of pleasure sailing craft. Quite unabashedly, he wrote of his apprenticeship at the Herreshoff Manufacturing Company:

> *Until I was 27 my bedroom was next to the rooms my father used for drawing, model making, and experimenting. On the walls were models that represented nearly all of the history of American yachting since the eighteen sixties. When quite young (four or five years old), my father used to take me by the hand to inspect the work at the yacht yard. Here he deposited me in the row-boat shop. Soon I was running errands to the stockroom, and by six years of age was under pay working after school and on Saturdays. As the years went by I was riveting, bending frames, planning. At ten I knew all the woods by sight and was a good judge of timber for bending. Later I served my time, or worked for a time, in the pattern shop, the foundry, blacksmith shop, machine shop, boiler shop, mold loft, sail loft, rigging loft, the steel construction ship, wood construction shop, drafting room and the office.*

During World War I, young L. Francis Herreshoff designed underwater shapes for the navy, and he later worked for W. Starling Burgess. By 1925 he was designing yachts on his own, "for most every important class which has raced in the country." L. Francis not only designed racing yachts, but he also created cruising yachts, canoes and small sailing craft. His interests and experience were as broad as the yachting industry. In the 1940s he began writing his famous articles for *Rudder Magazine*. These articles formed the basis for subsequent books: *The Common Sense of Yacht Design*, *Capt. Nat Herreshoff*, *The Complete Cruiser* and *Introduction to Yachting*. In essence, L. Francis Herreshoff's life, and this collection of his published accumulated knowledge, chronicles the golden age in American yachting. Current and future generations are indeed fortunate that he sensed a need to preserve the record of his thoughts and activities.

ALGERNON SIDNEY DEWOLF HERRESHOFF (1890–1977)

A lifelong resident of Bristol, A. Sidney "Sid" DeWolf Herreshoff died at the age of ninety; he is remembered by sailors everywhere as a designer and yachtsman in a class by himself. He took over where his father, Captain Nat, left off and designed such boats as the *Fisher's Island 23*, the *Amphicraft Dinghy* and the experimental catamaran *Sea Spider*, a boat that featured a cockpit that could also be used as a tender.

Sid was survived by two sons, Nathanael G. Herreshoff III of Westampton, New Jersey, and Halsey C. Herreshoff of Bristol, who is also a naval architect and current president of the Herreshoff Marine Museum. Sid had four brothers: A. Griswold Herreshoff of Delray Beach, Florida; Clarence DeWolf Herreshoff of Bristol; L. Francis Herreshoff; and Nathanael G. Herreshoff Jr.

Sid is buried at the Juniper Hill Cemetery in Bristol.

OBITUARY OF A. SIDNEY DEWOLF HERRESHOFF

The following is Sid's obituary as reported in the *Bristol Phoenix*, dated May 12, 1977.

A. Sidney DeWolf Herreshoff, a well known yacht designer, died Saturday in Coconut Grove, Florida. The husband of Rebecca (Chase) Herreshoff, he was 90 years old.

A lifelong resident of this town, Mr. Herreshoff was born here on Nov. 22, 1886, son of the late Nathanael Greene Herreshoff, the famous yacht designer who founded the Herreshoff Manufacturing Company, formerly located in this town, and Clara (DeWolf) Herreshoff.

He attended Bristol schools, and graduated from the Massachusetts Institute of Technology in 1911. As an engineer and designer, he was for many years chief naval architect of the Herreshoff Manufacturing Company, builders of America's Cup defenders and many of the world's foremost sail and power yachts. After the closing of the company in 1946, he worked as a self-employed naval architect, continuing in private practice until his death.

A 43 foot yacht of his design recently completed a round the world cruise and two of his designs are currently under construction in Rhode Island. He was widely consulted on matters concerning the history and design of yachts.

Mr. Herreshoff was president of the Herreshoff Marine Museum, an honorary life member of the Bristol Yacht Club, and a member of the Providence Engineering Society. He was also a member of the Bristol Historical and Preservation Society, was active for many years in YMCA in the town, and was formerly president of the Bristol Skating Club.

Mr. Herreshoff will be particularly remembered for his unique talents in sailing and in the design and construction of yachts.

In addition to his wife, he is survived by two sons, Nathanael G. Herreshoff III of Mount Holly, New Jersey, and Halsey C. Herreshoff of Bristol and Boston, also a naval architect, and two brothers, A. Griswold Herreshoff of Delray Beach, Fla, and Clarence DeWolf Herreshoff of this town: two grandsons, and two granddaughters.

The funeral was held yesterday at St. Michael's Church.

Canon Delbert W. Tildesley officiated, and read committal prayers at the Juniper Hill Cemetery.

Bearers were Griswold Boynton, Capt Harold Payson, Joseph G. Kinder, and Dudley Williams. Ushers were Douglas McCleod and Frank Pardee.

Herreshoff hull #321, under construction in 1917. Owner Payne Whitney of New York inquired of Assistant Secretary of the Navy F.D. Roosevelt what he might do to help the war effort. It was suggested that he might contract for a sub-chaser to be later purchased by the U.S. Navy. Herreshoff hull #321 was taken and commissioned on March 24, 1918. *Courtesy United States Navy.*

Herreshoff hull #306 revving her engines at the boatyard piers in Bristol Harbor. Built in 1917, this 112-foot-5-inch steel-hulled steamboat was acquired by the navy on February 14, 1918. She was loaned to the War Department from October 1920 to March 1921, and she was sold on December 1, 1922. This class was designed by A. Sidney DeWolf Herreshoff specifically for patrol service in World War I. *Courtesy United States Navy.*

Herreshoff hull #309 running trials with U.S. Navy crew aboard. This eighty-three-foot-two-inch A. Sidney DeWolf Herreshoff–designed steam patrol boat was built in 1917 and acquired by the navy on August 1, 1917. She was commissioned on November 15, 1917, and returned to her owner on January 11, 1919. *Courtesy United States Navy.*

Another view of A. Sidney DeWolf Herreshoff–designed hull #309. This steam patrol boat is running trials in Narragansett Bay with a U.S. Navy crew aboard. She was built expressly for shore patrol duty during World War I. *Courtesy United States Navy.*

Civilian workers and navy inspectors join designer A. Sidney DeWolf Herreshoff aboard hull #306 in Bristol Harbor. Herreshoff also built three other steamers of this type specifically for patrolling the U.S. coast: hulls #308, #321 and #323. *Courtesy United States Navy.*

HALSEY CHASE HERRESHOFF (1933–PRESENT)

Halsey continues in the family's long history of naval architects and marine engineers. His education achievements, including a bachelor of science degree from the Webb Institute of Naval Architecture and a master's degree from the Massachusetts Institute of Technology, have adequately prepared him for his life's work. After a stint in the U.S. Navy, achieving the rank of lieutenant, he worked as a naval architect with Bethlehem Steel Company and taught at the Massachusetts Institute of Technology. As the grandson of Captain Nat and the son of Sidney, who designed yachts for the former Herreshoff Manufacturing Company, Halsey carries on the traditional interests of the family. Additionally, Halsey has taken on the role of a spirited public servant; before his current election to his sixth term on the Bristol Town Council, he acted as the town's elected chief executive officer (town administrator) from 1986 to 1994.

Halsey C. Herreshoff. *Author's collection.*

Halsey enjoys a distinguished career as a designer of boats, with more than ten thousand vessels built to his designs; he has been called to provide engineering consultation to government, industry and private clients.

He, like his brethren of days long past, is an avid sailor and respected navigator. His experience and knowledge of the finer points of ocean racing is unchallenged. His experiences are enviable; he was a member of the crew of the 1958 America's Cup defender *Columbia*, and navigator in three additional America's Cup defenses: *Courageous* in 1974, *Freedom* in 1980 and *Liberty* in 1983.

Aboard his vintage Herreshoff-built New York forty-foot yawl *Rugosa*, Halsey completed a 25,000-mile cruise in European waters, where he placed first in the vintage class of the America's Cup Jubilee and in the Mediterranean races. Halsey remains active, heading Herreshoff Designs, and he is president of the Herreshoff Marine Museum and the America's Cup Hall of Fame.

A corner of one of the Herreshoff storage buildings

STORAGE

Your yacht deserves the protection of the Herreshoff steel-framed, scientifically lighted and ventilated storage building in which full precautions have been taken against fire and theft. Besides day and night watchman service, the entire property is protected by a seven-foot chain link fence. The yard is serviced by two fire hydrants, sand-filled fire pails and chemical appliances.

View of Herreshoff storage basin and yards

Years of experience in the building of the finest yachts insure your boat the treatment of sympathetic and intelligent artisans.

The Herreshoff storage agreement specifically provides for all contingencies. We particularly stress the fact that it anticipates cost, present and future, and obviates the usual irritating extra charges. For your convenience there is a choice

Quoting from a recent report made by E. D. Wright, of the Bureau for the Prevention of Explosion and Fire on Motor Boats, "Making a tour of this plant, I found it in perfect order, in fact, the best kept and cleanest plant I have ever had the pleasure of inspecting. I think it only due to Mr. Haffenreffer to say that out of the fifty-three yards visited, this yard and shops are in the best condition." of either wet storage, storage under canvas, or storage under roof. All these types are available at rates comparable to the quality of the service provided.

Our service department will gladly quote prices on receipt of overall length, beam and draft. Please specify type of yacht, number and type of batteries, etc. Address Box 3, Bristol, R. I.

Herreshoff **BRISTOL R.I. U.S.A.**

Author's collection.

CHAPTER 6

SHIPSHAPE 'N' BRISTOL FASH'N

"Shipshape 'n' Bristol Fash'n" might easily be applied to the mariners and ship builders of Narragansett Bay. These four words are the highest compliment a sailor can pay to those who had set a standard of seamanship certain to be found on Bristol-built and Bristol-sailed boats. For while Bristol, England, was a famous sailing ship place, so Bristol, Rhode Island, is famous as a yachting center. The passing of years has not lessened the interest of the American Bristol-made boats in bright paint, clean bottoms and well-scraped spars, taut rigging, neatly coiled lines and perfectly set sails.

When the words "Ship shape 'n' Bristol fash'n" are spoken in any of the world's ports, the listener instantly knows of which Bristol, of the world's many, the speaker is referring.

John Brown was encouraged by the commission of distinguished yachtsman Thomas Clapham to build a boat for him along the lines of the *Kelpie*. With several more orders on file, the young J.B. secured the Old Tannery building situated on the east shore of Bristol Harbor for use as a boat shop. He hired a few men and started to fill the orders. Starting from 1866, the yard became widely known to the world's mariners. The yard only built sailing vessels until 1868, when the first steamer, the *Annie Morse*, was laid down. The next steamer, the *Seven Brothers*, was built for the Church brothers of Tiverton, Rhode Island; this vessel had the distinction of being the pioneer fishing steamer on the Atlantic Coast. For these two vessels, the engines and other machinery were procured elsewhere. But for the next steam launch, the *Anemone*, the plans and designs were made by Nat, who was then employed by the Corliss Steam Engine Company. Using his brother's plans, J.B. built the engine in his Bristol shop.

In 1878, Nathanael joined his fortunes with his brother John. Each man was a genius in his discipline. From that point on the enterprise grew in size and importance, all the while leading the way in improved methods of yacht design and construction. As a designer Nathanael had no peer. Prominent yachtsmen regarded his craftsmanship and that of those who he employed to be unexcelled. A long period of steam vessel construction, during which many experiments of inestimable value were made with engines and boilers, was followed with a return to the building of sailing craft.

With growth of the yard and increasing interest in boats designed and built by Herreshoff, it was evident that Bristol had lost none of its age-old distinction and heritage of a reputation made upon the sea.

The Herreshoffs resolved to turn out only yachts of the highest quality. To retain skilled craftsmen they paid about the highest wage in the state. This did induce good men to come to the company, but most of the workmen came because they wanted to be associated with the Herreshoff name, which symbolized the highest standard in construction and skilled craftsmanship. The yachts that the Herreshoff plant turned out were of such a high quality that the workmen could not help but feel pride in their workmanship. As a result, a great many of those men made lifelong careers at the Herreshoff Manufacturing Company.

At the Burnside and Hope Street Herreshoff boatyard, boys grew into men in the shops. Training in those long, rambling sheds became a privilege to the youths in whose blood was the strong flavor of the sea. Masters of every phase of the art of shipbuilding passed on to their sons the technique of fashioning spars, carving planks, caulking seams, splicing stays and cutting sails. The Herreshoff Manufacturing Company was an organization of specialists who relished the fascinating and intricate art that generations have directly inherited. The preeminence of the Herreshoff products on the world's seas attests to this unique adherence to an ideal.

CHAPTER 7

GENEALOGY OF THE *GLORIANA*

The cat yawl is a Bristol variety of boat. Not that there are no cat yawls anywhere else, but at Bristol they flourished.

In late summer 1890, a sail in the *Clara* convinced E.D. Morgan, a leading yachtsman of the time, to order two improved cat yawls from the Herreshoff Yard: the *Pelican* (Hull #408) and the *Gannet* (Hull #409). Both of these cat yawls incorporate improvements of the *Clara*. They were both of the same design, except that the *Gannet* was three feet longer than the *Pelican*. The objective was to determine the difference in sailing performance with the longer waterline.

As the result, the *Pelican* was launched in December 1890, and on the seventh of that month the designer and his brother, Lewis, made a trial trip in her, although the gale into which they sailed was one of the severest of the winter. The craft proved stiff and fast, and it was seen at once that her model was a success. This particular boat is important because the *Gloriana*, the much-heralded champion racer in the history of the sport, was the direct outgrowth of the *Pelican*.

There is a direct line of progression from the *Consuelo* and the *Clara* to the *Pelican* and the *Gannet*, and then to the successful 1891 "forty-six footer" the *Gloriana*, which revolutionized racing yacht design with her overhanging bow, cut-away forefoot and scientifically engineered rig.

In a letter dated March 6, 1932, Captain Nat wrote, "In underwater type she [the *Consuelo*] was the forerunner of *Gloriana* but not as to above water."

Carlton J. Pinheiro in his book, *Recollections*, quotes the following by Captain Nat: "These [the *Pelican* and the *Gannet*] were the first I had designed with an overhanging bow and I was so impressed with the advantages, I used the principle in the extreme in designing *Gloriana* the following year."

TIMING MADE THE DIFFERENCE

After the *Volunteer* soundly defeated the *Thistle* in the 1887 duel for the Cup, and before the next challenge was announced, a new intelligence in yacht designing had arisen and

The busy north shed; in construction is the *Pelican* in the foreground and the *Vamoose* in the background, 1891. *Courtesy Herreshoff Marine Museum.*

a new type of boat had come into being. Nat Herreshoff picked up the designer's pencil where Edward Burgess had laid it at his death.

Author William E. Simmons offered the contemporaneous opinions of yachtsmen on the *Gloriana* in his article "A Chapter of Yachting Development," published in *Frank Leslie's Monthly* of July 1899. Simmons writes that in the summer of 1891, Captain Nat sailed an odd-looking sloop into New York waters. Though only forty-six feet on the water line, she was seventy feet overall. At first yachtsmen laughed at her long, pig-shaped nose and flaring, convex bows, but then they marveled at her sailing qualities. Nothing in her class could keep within sight of her. This was the *Gloriana*'s coming out party. The *Gloriana* proved to be a revolution in yachting.

Captain Nat's revolutionary yacht, the *Gloriana*; this forty-five-foot-three-inch cutter of 1891 was the forerunner of the modern sail racing yacht. From the *Gloriana* model came the 1893 Cup defender *Vigilant*. *Courtesy Herreshoff Marine Museum.*

This is the *Dido*, a sixty-foot steam launch built in 1881; it is typical of the steam launches built at the Herreshoff Manufacturing Company in the last part of the nineteenth century. *Courtesy of Herreshoff Marine Museum.*

CHAPTER 8

THE *GLORIANA'S* VICTORY WAS CAPTAIN NAT'S TRIUMPH

Mr. E.D. Morgan recommended the Herreshoff shops to Royal Phelps Carroll, who was intending to build a boat for the season of 1891, and the result was that the order for a forty-six-footer, the future *Gloriana*, was placed at Bristol. Meanwhile, Mr. Carroll married and went to Europe; this event changed his plans for the coming racing season to such an extent that the new yacht was ultimately constructed for Mr. Morgan.

It has been said that the *Gloriana* was a lucky accident, but those who are familiar with the care and thought that the designer put into her are aware that such a notion is entirely erroneous. Here was a turning point in the career of Captain Nat. If he failed to build a fast boat, it would be said of him that his forté was the construction of steam craft, and that it would be better that he stick to that branch of marine architecture in the future—at least so far as craft of large size were concerned. On the other hand, if he should produce a boat far and away superior to the existing vessels of her class, unlimited possibilities would open up before him. And that was precisely what he did. The *Gloriana* was a success from the start, winning eight races of the new New York Yacht Club forty-six-foot class. At the end of the season she was confessedly the swiftest and ablest boat of her size on this side of the ocean, if not in the world.

The launch of the famous craft took place early in May. Mr. Morgan arrived in Bristol in a special railroad car to witness the event, and several hundred people watched her as she glided into Bristol Harbor. While her model was seen to be peculiar, there was something about it that suggested speed even to the untrained eye. Her name was suggested by a line in Spenser's "Faerie Queene," that greater, glorious queen of fairyland. When she won the race against the *Beatrix* off Newport in August, her trophy was a beautiful silver cup designed and made by the Whiting Silver Company of Providence, on which a feminine figure was engraved, representing Her Majesty of the fairy race. The *Gloriana's* chief characteristics are her raking stem and overhang stern, which make her look very different, viewed broadside on, from the racing yachts of former days.

The season of 1891 will long be remembered for the series of races between the forty-six-footers. This class of yachts had succeeded, in natural sequence, the forty-footers, and the contests between them were among the most interesting in the history of the

At ninety feet waterline length, the Herreshoff-designed and -built *Columbia* was one of the largest and most impressive of all the America's Cup yachts. In 1901, after many trials against the *Constitution* and the *Independence*, the *Columbia* was again chosen to save the Cup for the New York Yacht Club.

sport. It is worthwhile to notice that among all the aspirants for honors, only one boat of any importance, the Burgess yacht *Beatrix*, was a centerboarder. On account of this fact it was desired, from the beginning of the season, that the *Gloriana* should encounter her; and as race after race occurred and they did not come together, the popular interest in their ultimate meeting increased. In the first race in which the *Gloriana* started, on June 16, she was pitted against the *Nautilus* and the *Mineola*. The regatta was under the auspices of the Atlantic Yacht Club. The Bristol craft beat the *Mineola*, her nearest competitor, by eight minutes and seventeen seconds. Two days later, in the New York Yacht Club regatta, there were six starters, but the *Gloriana* won from all her rivals. Two of the contestants were designed by Burgess, two were Fife boats and a fifth was from the Wintringham shops. But the *Gloriana*, that Herreshoff wonder, beat her nearest competitor to the finish by a full half an hour. In this race there were ample wind and rain, the breeze blowing at the rate of twenty miles an hour.

The Seawanaka Corinthian Yacht Club regatta over the lower bay course off New York occurred on June 20, 1891. A heavy mist overspread the water, and the yachts were invisible at even a short distance. The rivals in this race were the *Nautilus* (Intringham), *Jessica* (Fife) and the *Gloriana*; the *Jessica* got away nearly two minutes ahead of the Bristol boat, but the latter soon forged to the front and ultimately won. On the succeeding Monday, the *Sayonara*—another Burgess craft—the *Jessica* and the *Uvira* contested with the *Gloriana* and were handily beaten. And on Tuesday, in a light breeze, the undefeated yacht won a fifth time, securing a handsome cup valued at $500, which had been offered as a prize by Vice Commodore David Banks of the Atlantic Yacht Club.

In this dramatic 1899 biograph photo image, the *Columbia* is running away from the *Shamrock I*, owned by Sir Thomas Lipton and representing the Royal Ulster Yacht Club.

In these races, Captain Nat was constantly in evidence, and a large degree of the success of the boat may be attributed to his wise seamanship, although in later seasons, without his presence, she continued her former successful record. In her sixth race, on August 7, for the Goelet Cup off Newport, the *Gloriana* won again; and on August 13 she secured another $500 trophy by defeating all the other boats of her class in a race designed especially for the forty-six-footers, though her margin on this occasion was only twenty-eight seconds. But as yet the *Beatrix*, which had been winning races in eastern waters, had not made her appearance against the Herreshoff boat, so that when the two finally met in the *Gloriana's* eighth race off Newport on August 17 popular interest was at its height. Captain Nat was again at the helm, and again the celebrated craft crossed the finish line a winner, beating the Burgess boat *Oweene* by a little more than a minute and the *Beatrix* by more than five minutes. This was the only time that the two rivals met during the season; but it was sufficient to give the *Gloriana* the undisputed championship in her class. She had won eight straight races, and in so doing had called general attention to her designer.

We further read in *Recollections* these words by Captain Nat.

> *While sailing her* [the Gloriana], *I conceived* Dilemma, *and had her built and tried her out that fall and* [the] *following year. From the success of* Gloriana, *we built* Wasp

the following winter, for the same class, and for Mr. Archibald Rogers. Wasp *was a little faster than* Gloriana. *Late in 1892, we had an order from Royal P. Carroll for an 85 ft. cruising sloop, in which he intended to cruise abroad and do some racing there. Late in that fall, there was a challenge for the America's Cup and quite promptly Archibald Rogers and others gave us an order for* Colonia, *which was specified to be keel and not over 14' draft. Mr. E.D. Morgan and others, believing these restrictions unwise, at [the] beginning of 1893, gave us an order for* Vigilant.

The victories of the *Gloriana*, coupled with the death of Edward Burgess in 1891, immediately elevated Captain Nat to the forefront of American designers, and led to his six successful defenses of the America's Cup.

The Burgess-designed *Rainbow* was the only American class-J yacht built in 1934. The *Rainbow*'s standing rigging, of high tensile steel rods, caused considerable discussion. *Courtesy* Yachting Magazine.

CHAPTER 9

HERRESHOFF'S SWIFT SAILORS

During his long years of work building boilers, engines and hulls for steam yachts, Captain Nat was by no means uninterested in sailing craft. He kept storing up ideas for future development, and no doubt he felt that at some time he would have an opportunity to turn to the construction of a sailing yacht of sufficient size to bring him into the first rank among the designers of such boats. He had been known before as a successful sailboat designer; his boat the *Shadow* of the early seventies had taken more prizes, perhaps, than any other sailing craft ever built. But there is a certain prestige attached to the construction of a successful big yacht that does not attach to the construction of smaller racing vessels.

Edward Burgess's name became widely known for the first time when he created his fast ninety-footer, although he had been building fast boats for a good many years. Nat Herreshoff yearned, without doubt, for the time when he would be able to show the world what he could do with a big racer of modern design. And as all things come to him who waits, this opportunity at length arrived. Now that the Herreshoffs had attained a reasonable competence level, the designer was able to give as much time as he desired to the development of any notion that may come into his head, though it ought to be added that in the case of the *Defender* the notion pays very well.

John B. Herreshoff was a shrewd businessman, and he had been more concerned with putting something aside for a rainy day than winning glory for himself or his brother by building swift sailing vessels. Then as today, there is good money spent for the construction of big sailing yachts.

It is said that when a yacht was needed to meet the *Genesta* in 1885, J.B. Herreshoff was approached and asked for figures on such a boat. The price he set was $30,000, as the story goes, and the prospective purchasers, considering the amount too high, placed their order with Edward Burgess, who designed the *Puritan* for them. What seems strangest about this story is that $30,000 should have been regarded as too great a price to pay for an America's Cup defender. The Vanderbilt-Iselin-Morgan syndicate would pay out many times greater than that amount when they settled for the new aluminum and bronze vessel from Bristol.

In 1890, the *Gloriana* was built for Commodore E.D. Morgan from Herreshoff designs and she proved to be an overwhelmingly successful racing yacht. The following year the first yacht with a metal plate keel and heavy lead bulb was built at the yard, beginning an era of fin-keel construction. New orders for large yachts were soon received and then, during the winter of 1892–93, the company went to work on two trial sloops for the international races with Great Britain for the defense of the America's Cup.

Both sloops, the *Colonia* and the *Vigilant*, were launched in the spring of 1893. In the trials, the *Vigilant* proved superior to her sister sloop and was entered as the defender of the Cup in the international race, which she won handily. The *Vigilant* was the first of an unbroken line of victorious defenders of the America's Cup built in Bristol, a line whose unvarying success has carried the name of Herreshoff to all the yachting capitals of the world.

The challenge of the *Valkyrie* for 1893 brought out three new boats, the *Vigilant*, *Colonia* and *Pilgrim*. The *Vigilant* and the *Colonia* were built by the Herreshoffs, the last by a Boston firm. The *Vigilant* was a centerboard, and the *Colonia* was a keel yacht. The struggle for the honor of defending the Cup was confined to the two Bristol-built boats, which were of the same type in the upper body as the *Gloriana*. The Boston boat could not keep pace with Captain Nat's flyers. The *Volunteer*, which, having been changed to a schooner and re-rigged as a sloop "as a trial horse," made only a poor showing alongside the Herreshoff creations. The *Vigilant*, built of Tobin bronze for strength and

The tenth race for the America's Cup brought out a new yacht designed by Captain Nat, called the *Defender*. The *Defender* won three races: the first in an extremely light wind, fouled in the second and the third by default. *Author's collection.*

Five seconds after the foul of the *Defender* (right) by the *Valkyrie III*, September 10, 1895. *Author's collection.*

The *Defender* rounds the mark with plenty of room. The *Vigilant* (1893), *Defender* (1895) and *Columbia* (1899 and 1901) were all Herreshoff creations. The *Reliance* followed on the heels of their success, forming a classic example of the fact that in most yacht development classes the successful boats get progressively bigger, heavier and more powerful. *Author's collection.*

lightness, showed herself to be a better all around boat and was therefore chosen to meet the challenger.

After the passage of two years, the *Defender* came out of the Herreshoff yards. Thanks to the inventive genius of Captain Nat, this racing sloop of ninety-foot waterline sported many improvements and novelties in both hull design and rigging. Four years later, the *Columbia* was launched and was victorious in both the 1899 and 1901 Cup races with Great Britain. The *Reliance* followed in 1903, and then there was the long interval before the *Resolute* sailed to victory in 1920. For the races in 1930, two flyers—the *Weetamoe* and the *Enterprise*—were constructed at the Herreshoff yard under the supervision of the company's new owners, the Haffenreffer family. The *Enterprise* was chosen to defend the Cup, and she easily won four of the seven races against Sir Thomas Lipton's *Shamrock V* in Rhode Island Sound.

THE *VIGILANT'S* SUCCESS
From the *Bristol Phoenix*, October 21, 1893:

> The *Vigilant's* success is Bristol's, for this is the birthplace of the yacht that outsails the world and brings fame to her designers.
>
> "Nat Herreshoff won't give a fellow a chance to win" was the disgusted comment of one of Capt. Nat's old time adversaries.
>
> Our amiable and sportsman like visitor Lord Dunraven probably feels about that way himself.
>
> New York is boasting now of her first victory in the international contest since Genesta *came over. For it was a Boston* [built] *boat that beat* Galatea *and a Boston boat that beat* Thistle. *As in the former competitions to select a defender for the America's Cup, Boston's* Volunteer *had no competitor to meet* Thistle*—The New York* [Yacht Club] *boats were built in New York.*
>
> This year New York came to Bristol for a boat and the result was Vigilant *and* Colonia, *two of the dandiest flyers that the world has ever known. The* Phoenix *rises to remark that it is proud of the fact it hails from the same town as Nat Herreshoff.*

THE *VIGILANT* BATTLES ON
From the *Bristol Phoenix*, July 28, 1894:

> It matters not as to whether the Vigilant, *in which our citizens take so much interest, be a winner or loser in the number of races over the other side of the water, it will not detract from the splendid victories heretofore won by the Herreshoffs in the numerous races in which the English sportsmen have met their crack yachts and been defeated.*
>
> Yet it must be recollected that although the Herreshoffs are the builders of the Vigilant, *she is owned by a gentleman who never was a true sportsman. It is* [Jay] *Gould, the owner, who is the loser or winner. Let the Prince of Wales bring the* Britannia *to Newport next season and if there is not more than an even score in the settlement won by*

the Yankees in their own waters, then they will settle down to the fact that "Britannia rules the waves," but not until then. There is no doubt that the Vigilant *has been handicapped in every way and it is doubtful if she is in as fine a racing trim as she was last season. Then taking into consideration the perfect understanding they have of the tides that prevail in those waters, it must be conceded that there is a chance of her being beaten by an English skipper whose experience is unquestioned.*

THAT *VIGILANT* AGAIN
From the *Bristol Phoenix*, August 11, 1894:

The last few races of the Vigilant *seem to have proved satisfactory to the average Bristolian, that in an open sea with equal chances, the* Britannia *is no match for her, provided there is wind enough to fill her canvass, and with the fair-minded English sportsman she is rated as being the fastest boat of her kind in* [her home] *waters.*

It is not a wonder that they rate Mr. Herreshoff as the greatest designer in the yacht building line in the world. A New York Herald *correspondent gives an interview with a prominent member of the Royal Victoria Yacht Club as follows:*

"I look upon it that the Vigilant *is a wonderfully designed boat, for she travels better on her side than she does on a level keel. She does not stand up to the wind like the* Britannia, *and that very lack of stiffness seems to favor her, for the further she heels the faster she seems to go. In fact, she never appears to get her full way on until she is well over on her side. I look upon it that her bronze bottom, which is like the glass of a watch, is of great advantage to her. If I were going to order a boat to beat the world, I would go to Mr. Herreshoff."*

THE *DEFENDER*
From the *Bristol Phoenix*, 1895:

While the new yacht Defender *has been in process of construction at Bristol, Rhode Island, public attention has been attracted in no small measure to that town and to the man who has designed and built the craft. It is only a few years ago that Edward Burgess was regarded as the greatest yacht designer of the day; and when he died, in 1891, the prediction was freely made that his equal would not soon be developed. Other men might be found who would design fast yachts, but the chances were that if the British yachtsmen should challenge for the America's trophy again, the cup would presently be on its way to the other side of the ocean. At least that was the conclusion at which a great many pessimistic observers arrived when they learned of the untimely death of the man who had created the* Puritan, *the* Mayflower, *and the* Volunteer. *But almost at the moment of Mr. Burgess's death the victories of the* Gloriana *were pointing unmistakably to Nat Herreshoff as the designer upon whom the task of producing another international champion might profitably be imposed.*

The launching of a Cup defender was a grand occasion in Bristol and many of the townsfolk flocked to the Hope Street seawall to cheer the yacht's debut. This photo engraving from the September 1895 issue of *Munsey's Magazine* illustrates the introduction of the *Defender.*

THE *DEFENDER* RETURNS TO BRISTOL
From the *Bristol Phoenix*, 1898:

> The Defender *will be put in first class shape for the trial races.*
>
> *Capt. John Terry of Fall River, with his workmen, pile-driver and other paraphernalia, arrived here Tuesday afternoon for the purpose of extending the ways at the Herreshoff shops out into the harbor a distance of about 290 feet. The work was begun Wednesday and is to be completed as soon as possible, so that* Defender, *which is now at Glen Island [New York], may be brought here and completely overhauled and put in good shape as a trial horse for the defense of the [America's] cup.*
>
> *The ways that were put down to launch* Defender *upon were taken up some time ago, and new ways will be put down nearly the entire length of 290 feet from the west end of the south construction shop. The distance beyond the end of where the ways were located for the launching of* Defender *is about 140 feet.*
>
> *The* Defender's *topsides will be removed, and it is understood that a thicker plating of aluminum will replace the plating now on, the present aluminum plating being more or less corroded.*
>
> *New deck beams of aluminum will also be substituted for the beams now in this yacht, which are of aluminum, and which are also corroded. The work of overhauling the* Defender *will be a long and slow job, and it is expected that the yacht will not be ready to go overboard until well into the spring.*

CHAPTER 10

THE J BOATS
(1930–1937)

The J class was adopted for America's Cup competition in 1928, looking forward to the next regatta in 1930. The class itself, though, dated back to the turn of the century, when the Universal Rule was adopted.

There no longer remain many Bristolians who have memories of trips to lower Hope Street, in the early 1930s, to see the J boats lined up in dry dock along Bristol Harbor's shore. They were the largest, most exciting and most beautiful sailing yachts in the history of competitive racing; alas, the J boats had a very short life. They were built from 1930 to 1937, ten in all, and then they vanished from the sports scene forever, the victims of their cost to design and build, the increase in federal taxes and the approach of World War II.

Still, for those seven short years what a magnificent show the J boats put on. It was a holiday in Bristol when one of these craft was launched. And in the summers of 1930 and 1937, Bristol became one of the tourist capitals of the Northeast as people flocked to the town to catch a glimpse of the J boats.

During the winter the J boats, the "peacocks" of the competing international sailing community, remained in Bristol, their canvas coverings giving them the appearance of huge prehistoric beasts. More than any other sailing craft built before or since, the J-class yachts had captured the imagination of the American public.

There were only ten J-class yachts designed and built: six in the United States and four in the United Kingdom. The original "greyhounds of the sea" were the *Enterprise*, the *Whirlwind*, the *Yankee*, the *Weetamoe* and the *Shamrock V*, all built in 1930. In 1933 the British *Velsheda* came out; the *Endeavour* and the *Rainbow* were built in 1934, and finally in 1937 the last of the J-rated yachts, the *Ranger* and the *Endeavour II*, were launched.

Additionally, several yachts of closely related dimensions, mostly twenty-three-meter International Rule boats, were converted after their construction to meet the rating rules of the J class.

The J boats defended the Cup three times: *Enterprise* defeated *Shamrock V* in 1930; *Rainbow* edged out *Endeavour* in six exciting match races in 1934; and the last of the Js, *Ranger*, swept *Endeavour II* in 1937.

The America's Cup defender *Enterprise* as seen on September 2, 1930, only a few days before the 1930 struggle for the Cup. The *Enterprise*, designed by W. Starling Burgess and built by the Herreshoff Manufacturing Company, sailed against Lipton's *Shamrock V.* The *Enterprise* won four races in rapid order, and never once was the outcome in doubt. *Courtesy Associated Press.*

SOMETHING ABOUT THE J BOATS

Ever since 1881, when the Canadians made their second attempt to lift the Cup from the New York Yacht Club (NYYC), each new challenge brought out at least one new yacht especially designed and built for the purpose of defending the most prestigious of sailing trophies.

In answer to Sir Thomas Lipton's challenge of 1929, the Americans designed four J-class yachts as possible defenders. The *Enterprise*, *Whirlwind*, *Yankee* and *Weetamoe* were launched within a month of each other; the *Weetamoe* and *Enterprise* from the Herreshoff yard in Bristol, and the *Yankee* and *Whirlwind* from Lawley & Son's yard in Neponset, Massachusetts.

Two of these, the *Weetamoe* and the *Yankee*, were trotted out again in 1934. During those trials the *Yankee* gave the new boat, the *Rainbow*, a considerable run for the right to defend. Both of the older boats had major alterations designed to increase their speed, and in the case of the *Yankee* the alteration was a distinct success.

Weetamoe was designed by Clinton H. Crane for a syndicate of NYYC members headed by Rear Commodore Junius S. Morgan Jr. and George Nichols. She was built

The *Rainbow* is launched from Herreshoff's south construction shed on May 15, 1934. The J-boat era of 1930 could be called the Vanderbilt era. Harold S. Vanderbilt was skipper in 1930, 1934 and 1937. He was also the principal backer of the magnificent Js *Enterprise*, *Rainbow* and *Ranger*, financing the latter entirely himself. *Author's collection.*

by the Herreshoff yard, and was one of the outstanding yachts of the year, giving the *Enterprise* the stiffest competition she met. She was fast in light to moderate air, but proved to be a bit weak when it blew hard. The previous winter, when she was hauled out at the Herreshoffs', her lead keel was removed, recast and lowered nearly two feet to give her added stability. A wooden filler was also fitted between the lead and the bronze keel casting. This, however, naturally increased her wetted surface and, as a result, her frictional resistance, a matter especially important in light weather.

In August, because of a rather dismal campaign, she was again taken back to Bristol and her lead was once more changed. *Weetamoe* was the narrowest of the 1930 quartet and her original model shows rather slack bilges and full garboards, with a minimum of wetted surface and beautiful fore and aft lines. Her mast and rigging are duplicates of the *Rainbow*'s.

The *Yankee* was designed by Frank C. Paine for a Boston syndicate headed by John S. Lawrence; she was built by the George Lawley & Son Corporation of Neponset, Massachusetts. She was the widest of the 1930 fleet of Js and the most powerful in model; she was fast in a breeze and decidedly able. However, the *Yankee* did not carry herself as well as expected. During the winter she was towed to Lawley's, hauled out and her sections from amidships to the bow were altered in shape. These changes made a new boat out of her and she was good in light to moderate air, and she did not stop when bucking into a sea. Her speed also improved. She carried the same hollow wooden mast she used in 1930.

The contenders to become the Cup defender *Rainbow* and *Weetamoe* (in background) start from the Brentons Reef Lightship in Rhode Island Sound, beginning their race to prove their strength to defend the Cup. *Author's collection.*

The *Rainbow*, the only new J built for the 1934 struggle, was designed by W. Starling Burgess, whose *Enterprise*, which was built in Bristol by the Herreshoffs, defended the Cup in 1930.

Rainbow's model was one of the most handsome of the four aspiring defenders. Forward, at the extreme bow, there was a pronounced flare in the topsides that gave additional room on deck. She also carried a small centerboard. A most novel feature introduced on this boat was her standing rigging, which was of high tensile heat-treated steel rods, connected by turnbuckles, instead of the usual wire rope. There were only two of these to a side, one leading to the lower spreaders and the other to a point some twenty-eight feet below the truck over the ends of the three spreaders. Her mast was of duralumin and pear-shaped in section, with the track for the slides of the mainsail fitted in the groove in her after part; it was about thirty inches fore and aft and eighteen athwart ships.

All three of the American boats were bronze plated on steel frames except the *Rainbow*, whose plating above the waterline was of steel. According to the rules in place at the time for the class, all winches were on deck, instead of being below. The deck-mounted winches made room below for quarters for all hands to live aboard rather than on tenders. Spare sails and gear, however, were still stowed on tenders or ashore.

OLD J-CLASS BOATS NEVER DIE

Out of ten America's Cup Js, only two survive today: *Shamrock V*, the 1930 challenger, and *Endeavour*, the 1934 challenger. The *Velsheda*, distinguished by being the only yacht built as a J class but not intended for America's Cup, is intact and sailing, too. Of at least seven other boats that were rated as Js, two remain: the *Cambria* and *Astra*. *Cambria* was originally a twenty-three-meter International Rule yacht, but later altered to rate as a J. The surviving boats have all had extensive restoration and rebuilding. *Endeavour* was rescued from near oblivion, as she was too delicate to move without structural reconstruction.

The *Ranger* was broken up in 1941. Her small stern is displayed in the *Endeavour*'s saloon since she was restored by Elizabeth Meyer in 1989. A replica of the *Ranger* was launched at the Danish Yachts shipyard in Skagen, Denmark, in 2004.

By 1946 all of the American yachts were laid up, and later scrapped for their metal. None survived. The *Endeavour* and *Velsheda* were houseboats on the Hamble River. This is where they stayed for more than thirty years, protected by the mud berth in which they had sunk. Only the *Shamrock V* was still sailing.

The historic 1934 America's Cup entry, the *Endeavour*, was purchased in September 2006 for $13.1 million by Diversicolor Ltd., a Cayman Islands corporation owned by forty-four-year-old investor Mr. Cassio Antunes, a resident of Hawaii. Antunes has restored the British "Red Ensign" flag on the *Endeavour*. He said his family wants to race the sloop again against the two other J-class yachts built in the 1930s, the *Shamrock V* and the *Velsheda*.

Elizabeth Meyer, president of J-Class Management, bought *Endeavour* in England in 1984 and spent five years and $10 million restoring her before selling to L. Dennis Kozlowski for $15 million in 2000. The *Endeavour* had not been sailed for almost half a century when Elizabeth found it.

YACHT	YEAR	LOA	LWL	BEAM	DRAUGHT	DISPLACE-MENT	BUILT
Enterprise	1930	120' 6"	50'	23'	14' 6"	126 tons	USA
Shamrock V	1930	119' 1"	81' 1"	20'	14' 9"	134 tons	UK
Weetamoe	1930	125' 9"	83'	20'	15'		USA
Whirlwind	1930	130'	86'	21' 9'	15' 6"		USA
Yankee	1930	126'	83'	22' 6"	14' 6"	148 tons	USA
Velsheda	1933	127' 6"	83'	21' 6"	15'		UK
Endeavour	1934	129' 6"	83' 6"	22'	14' 9"	143 tons	UK
Rainbow	1934	127' 6"	82'	21'	15'	141 tons	USA
Endeavour II	1937	135' 6"	87'	21' 6"	15'	162 tons	UK
Ranger	1937	135'	87'	21'	15'		USA

LOA=Overall Length   LWL=Load Waterline Length

CHAPTER 11

THE HERRESHOFFS AND THE MOTORCAR

In 1880, Captain Nat and his brother James built a steam-driven automobile. They pirated the boiler from a Stanley Steamer and after removing the engine from a Renault chassis installed the boiler and a three-cylinder engine of Nat's design. This engine was, in 1904, the basis for his revolutionary compound engine. Nat tinkered with the steamer's gasoline burner, and to get greater motive power the valve on the expansion tank was tightened.

Suddenly, disaster! The tank burst, spraying liquid fire on Nat's hands and arms. For many weeks he was in agonizing pain. It was feared he would never regain use of his hands and fingers. Though Nat regained full mobility and feeling in his hands and fingers, he never again drove or experimented with automobiles.

The Stanley brothers and the Herreshoff brothers were friendly. From this friendship, the Stanleys were on the receiving end of suggestions from the Herreshoffs of ways to improve their vehicle's engine. The improvements must have proved successful, because these changes were incorporated into future models.

J.B.'s avid interest in speed and automobiles led him to begin collecting several, to which he often made alterations. Several automobile companies had endorsements and photos of the famous boat builder in some of their advertisements.

J.B. loved speed and the idea of owning any new invention that would distinguish him as the fastest person in Bristol allured him. The automobile was to him the new symbol of stature and speed. His desire to own top-of-the-line motorcars was insatiable; in short order he purchased a Pierce Arrow, a model L Rambler and a Stanley Steamer. Polished to a high sheen and in top-notch running condition, he displayed them, lined up near the plant on Burnside Street.

One afternoon, on the west side of Narragansett Bay, the blind J.B. said to his driver, "You are lost, aren't you?"

The driver replied, "How did you know?"

J.B. said the road didn't feel right and that the sun was in the wrong direction. The driver asked, "How do I get back on the correct road?"

J.B. replied, "I will tell you." And proceeded to do just that.

THE HERRESHOFF MOTOR COMPANY OF CHARLES FREDERICK (1880–1954)

When brother James and his second son, the handsome Charles Frederick, returned to Bristol from California, which had lost its charm for them, James convinced J.B. to hire his nephew as an apprentice draftsman. Charles Frederick had his share of the family's proclivity for inventive ideas. He designed the sloop *San Toy* for his New York cousin, Francis Lee Herreshoff. J.B. examined the lines of the finished product and proclaimed the boat a failure. The craft, he proclaimed, was so beneath the standards of the company that he recommended it be scrapped.

Young Charles was so sure he had designed and built a superior vessel that he challenged his uncle Captain Nat to a race in Bristol Harbor against any boat of Nat's choosing. Captain Nat, in the *Kildee*, was badly beaten. Nat demanded a rematch; this time he was bested more soundly than in the initial match.

It was this Charles Frederick who inaugurated the manufacturing of a line of elegant, speedy family automobiles. In 1910, the newly incorporated Herreshoff Motor Company contracted the Lycoming Foundry and Machine Co. of Detroit, Michigan, to manufacture the engines for the Herreshoff National Champion, Model 25. The Herreshoff Motor Company's general offices and factory were located at 630 Harper Avenue, Detroit.

The 1911 Model 25, a four-passenger open (top optional) vehicle was widely advertised in the magazines *Motor Age* and *The Horseless Age* for sale at the relatively high price of $950. Other models available included a Touring Car, a Tourabout and a Runabout, each available for $1,500. The four-cylinder Herreshoff motor generated twenty-four horsepower; the selective sliding gear transmission was capable of three speeds ahead and reverse. The snappy color combination of Herreshoff Royal Blue with cream-colored running gear was the restricted combination available.

The illustrated display advertisement notified potential buyers that "all specifications [are] given in detail in our complete illustrated catalog which is mailed to you upon request."

Through the courtesy of the Herreshoff Marine Museum library, we are able to quote the following from the 1910 Herreshoff Motors Catalog.

The 1910 Herreshoff Car is offered to the public in its second year with increased confidence in the knowledge that there is a growing demand among discriminating motorists for a small car of the best class. It is not intended to appeal to the man who is seeking a low-priced product. It is designed to supply the need of those who appreciate the excellence and elegance of high-priced cars but who realize that most of these cars are bigger and more costly to maintain than the usual service they render, warrants. It is intended to be a smaller edition of the high-priced car. Bred of the same stock, as correct in design, as careful in workmanship and built of the same materials, the Herreshoff car is a typically a car of class as the highest-priced foreign car. And it will do the work ordinarily required of the big car with equal satisfaction while entailing a much smaller initial outlay, a smaller upkeep, and smaller operating expense.

Its economy in these respects was due solely to its design of motor, lightness, and even distribution of weight. Its lightness was obtained without any sacrifice of strength, by the use of good material. That all the parts were sufficiently heavy is proved by the fact that in no car was any structural weakness found. At the same time there was no excess weight in any part of its structure. Each component part was designed to suit every other part and all were so related as to form together a harmonious whole.

Then, with no little boasting, the catalogue's author goes to great lengths to espouse the talent and character of the automobile's designer, Charles Frederick Herreshoff, son of James.

There is no designer who is better qualified to produce a car that combines strength and lightness. Herreshoff, with his experience in yacht building, early learned the secret of reducing weight in construction. In yacht building the employment of the best material is essential to success. The yacht designer who is able to retain strength while reducing weight to a minimum is the successful constructer.

Mr. Herreshoff inherited mechanical genius from his father and acquired mechanical skill through association with great men. While abroad at college he built the 80 foot yacht Nevada *that won conspicuous victories in foreign waters. He built the yacht* Iroquois *that won the Canada Cup after he returned to America. He then took up the building of motor boats and his* Den I *and* Den II, *his* Vim, Alabama, *and* Vivien *have won wide renown for him by successes in their respective classes. He has never built a motor boat that has failed to win conspicuous victories.*

THE NOVARA

Just prior to World War I, the age of America's love affair with the automobile dawned. The Herreshoff men were no different from other wealthy Bristol young men who had a need for speed and sporty styling in their vehicles. There was in town a friendly competition among them in customizing their ubiquitous Model T Fords.

Sid Herreshoff and his father, Captain Nat, hatched an idea for a commercially built sports car. The prototype of this car, called the NOVARA, was built at the Herreshoff east shop at the corner of Hope and Burnside Streets. This famous company that owed its continuing fame to the perfection of streamline design in yacht construction used that knowledge in building the NOVARA. The result was a sleek, open-cockpit roadster.

Sid had two aims in his design: light weight and exceptional acceleration. He accomplished this by eliminating wind resistance and concentrating on balance. At approximately 1,500 pounds, it offered "25 to 32 miles per gallon of gasoline" at speeds ranging from 50 to 70 miles per hour.

A partnership was formed with Gorham N. Thurber in association with the Isotta Fraschini Motors Company, 2 West Fifty-seventh Street, New York. The estimated price of the special design sports car was $2,750, certainly a princely sum considering that a Ford runabout was selling for about $345 at this time.

Construction of the NOVARA began in the summer and fall of 1916, with the intent of it being the 1917 model. For a number of reasons, the model never went into production except for the single car produced, the principal reason being the market for this type of expensive speedy sports car had dried up as the young men it was geared to attract were off fighting in the trenches of the European war.

The NOVARA was driven by Sid for a number of years and eventually wound up on the New England auto racing circuit in the dirt track days of the Roaring Twenties.

Author's collection.

The fastest yacht in the world, the *Reliance*, spreads her wings in a trial run in Narragansett Bay. The *Reliance*'s specifications are: LWL (load waterline length), 89 feet; LOA (overall length), 149 feet; end of bowsprit to end of boom, 201 feet; sail area, 16,700 square feet; displacement, 100 tons; crew, 64. *Courtesy Herreshoff Marine Museum.*

CHAPTER 12

THE *RELIANCE,* WINNER OF THE AMERICA'S CUP IN 1903

They tell me I have a beautiful boat. I don't want a beautiful boat. What I want is a boat to lift the Cup—a Reliance. *Give me a homely boat, the homeliest boat that was ever designed, if she is as fast as* Reliance. *I want* Reliance.
–Sir Thomas Lipton after the failure of his Shamrock III, *designed by William Fife Jr.*

These were the kind of compliments toward what has become one of the most celebrated boats in the history of the America's Cup and its designer, Nathanael Greene Herreshoff.

But the massive scale of the 1903 defender frightened the America's Cup establishment, which would adopt, ten years later, a more conservative approach to the design and building of America's Cup yachts.

In 1903, the rule imposed only one major constraint on Herreshoff: the load waterline length of the boat couldn't exceed 27.43 meters. The designer modeled a flat and modestly deep hull, similar to that of a scow. The biggest surprise came from the long overhangs: 6.70 meters forward and 7.92 meters aft. Sailing close hauled, in seven or eight knots of breeze, the effective waterline length would stretch out from 27.43 meters to nearly 40 meters—a tremendous source of speed.

The one-hundred-ton lead keel, shaped like a fin, came down very deep. The boat would settle into a comfortable, fast heel very easily, possibly because Herreshoff managed to exploit the most improbably enormous sail area ever seen to that point on a single mast: a massive 16,700 square feet of canvas, approximately 186 square feet more than the *Shamrock III.*

Due to the scale of the boat, and the loads on it, Captain Nat fitted the *Reliance* with uncountable innovations: Tobin Bronze hull; steel-welded mast with a telescopic topmast sliding into the mainmast; two-speed winches; sheets and runners laid under an aluminum deck covered with cork; and a hollow rudder that could be filled or emptied of water depending on the point of sail. It would take all the effort and nautical wisdom of the incredible Charlie Barr to safely skipper the *Reliance* through the Cup, along with a crew of sixty-four.

Above: 1903, the twelfth race for the America's Cup, pitted the *Reliance*, the boat that was to become known as the fastest yacht in the world, against Lipton's *Shamrock III*. *Author's collection.*

Opposite: The *Reliance* was a powerful giant of a yacht with innumerable innovations of considerable interest. She completely outclassed all comers and won the Cup decisively. Arguably the greatest and most interesting of all Cup yachts, *Reliance* had a short career, being broken up soon after she so demonstrably fulfilled her mission of defending the Cup. *Author's collection.*

The simple fact that the *Reliance* was built and sailed is, on its own, an exceptional event in the history of the America's Cup. Behind this fantastic 1903 defender, there was a gallery of great men. Among them were Captain Nat, perhaps the best yacht designer of all time; Charlie Barr, among the most talented skippers in yachting history; and the money men behind the project, such as J.P. Morgan and John Rockefeller, who spent countless dollars to repel Sir Thomas Lipton's assault on the Cup. The *Reliance* remains a singular symbol. Better than any other boat, the *Reliance* expresses the logic of the all-or-nothing contest, sailed with intensity without equal, between two great rivals, Great Britain and America.

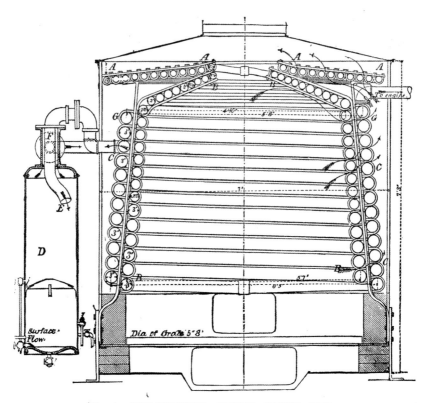

Fig. 3.—HERRESHOFF STEAM GENERATOR.

A cross section view of the Herreshoff coil boiler steam generator. *Courtesy* American-Scientific.

During the third and final race of the America's Cup match, sailed on September 3, 1903, on a twenty-mile windward-leeward course from the Sandy Hook lightship, a thick fog enveloped the racecourse. The *Reliance* had just turned, well ahead, when both boats disappeared from sight. Foghorns began a sinister concert, dominated by the siren on the lightship, which rang to indicate to the racers where the finish line might be found. The wait was long, and each spectator scrutinized the fog until the flapping of a sail in the wind could be heard and the *Reliance* appeared out of the mist like a ghost from the beyond. She crossed the finishing line to the acclaim of the crowd at 5:30 in the afternoon as the crew hauled in the enormous spinnaker in a superb display of seamanship. The *Shamrock III* lost its bearings in the fog that afternoon and eventually sailed directly to its mooring.

In the evening of its victory, just 146 days after its christening, the *Reliance* was laid up in dry dock. In an ironic twist, Lem Miller, the skipper of the *Columbia* who was beaten by Barr and the *Reliance* during the NYYC defender trials, led the 1903 winner to Robins Yard in South Brooklyn, in 1913, where she was scrapped.

CHAPTER 13

THE COIL BOILER

James and brother Nathanael collaborated in the conception and development of the famous Herreshoff safety coil boiler. Captain Nat gave much attention to the designing of the machinery for the steam craft he and his brother J.B. were building, and in the course of his long years of work and experiment, made many improvements in the engines with which they were equipped.

The earliest practical application of the coil boiler was the subject of a news item in the February 5, 1876 *Bristol Phoenix*:

THE NEW WATER WORKS

The new apparatus for furnishing water in the compact part of the town, in case of fire, is now nearly completed.

A trial of the pumps, pipes, coil boiler, etc., was made on Saturday last and gave great satisfaction to all interested.

A new pumping station has been erected on the west side of Thames Street, near the foot of John Street. The Herreshoff safety coil boiler, used for generating steam, is made of three inch steam pipe, about 550 feet in length of pipe. Inside of this long pipe coil the diameter is six feet; the smoke jacket is an outer casing of sheet iron.

In five and a half minutes from the time of lighting the fire, steam was generated. At nine and three quarter minutes the large pump was in full operation. The steam pressure was kept at about a hundred pounds and part of the time blowing off at the safety valve. The long length of pipe was quickly filled and eight lengths of hose were attached to hydrants more than half a mile away from the station, four of which were 1 and one quarter inches, and four of one inch, each playing [a stream of water] from 100 to 125 feet in height, and where these hydrants were situated, on Wood Street, is some forty feet above tide water.

The coil boiler is the largest of the kind ever made by the Herreshoff Manufacturing Company, and has proved a great success. Competent judges inform us that it is capable of furnishing 400 horsepower.

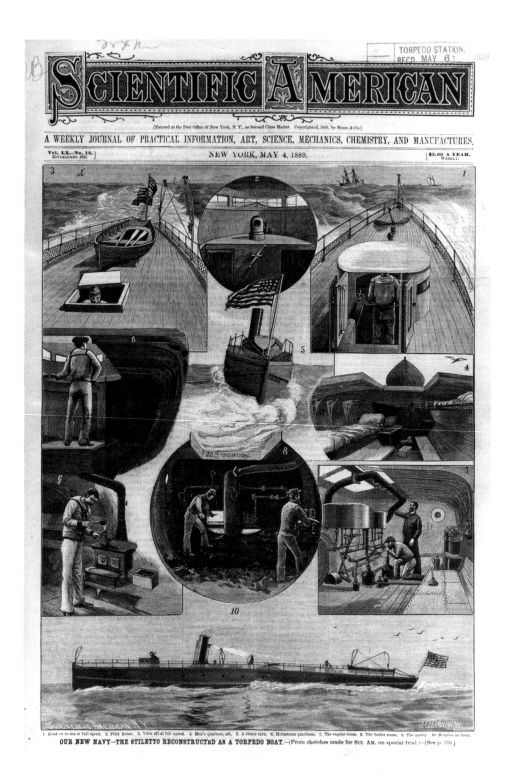

The May 4, 1889 issue of the weekly journal *Scientific American* introduced its subscribers to America's first self-propelled torpedo boat, the *Stiletto. Author's collection.*

CHAPTER 14

TORPEDO BOATS

SPAR TORPEDO BOATS

During the late 1870s until about 1883, Nat Herreshoff concentrated almost all of his attention on the development of light steam engines and on improving the construction of hulls, trying to reduce weight without sacrificing strength as an attempt to get into the booming military market for speedy torpedo boats. Practically all of this innovative work was being done in connection with the light steam launches the Herreshoff brothers were currently building and, although these early experiments were originally criticized by the brotherhood of yachtsmen, it is true that many of today's small boats are still built using the construction techniques worked out at the Herreshoff boatyard more than 130 years ago. Proof of Herreshoff's authority in the matter is the fact that so many of his small boats, although lighter in construction than those of his contemporary competitors, are still in use almost a century and a half later.

These small, fast, highly maneuverable, whale-backed, double-ender steam launches armed with SPAR torpedoes were built to be hoisted up on the davits of ships, so extreme lightness in both power plant and hull was paramount. The Herreshoff launches stood up better in service than heavier ones made by other boatyards. The reason for their superior service was twofold. When a launch comes alongside another vessel in a seaway, she will occasionally come in contact with the ship heavily, and in hoisting and lowering the launch there are unavoidable strains. The weight of a heavy launch makes these poundings and stresses more severe than with a light launch; the light launch with steam-bent frames will spring and give, cushioning the shock that will damage the unyielding, rigidly constructed boat with sawn frames.

The Herreshoffs built many of these early launches for several U.S. government agencies: the U.S. Navy, the Ordnance Department, the U.S. Coast Survey and the U.S. Fish Commission. One of their early models was twenty-two feet long and five feet three inches abeam. Built between 1876 and 1878, she represented the first attempt at the modern powerboat model. The greatest draft was a little aft of forefoot, and the greatest beam was near the stern, which was flat, the underwater shape being a gradual twist from bow to stern. These launches are said to have been very satisfactory, driving very easily into a moderate head sea. But Nathanael Herreshoff abandoned this model shortly after 1878, so we may assume that the sharp-bowed launches with wide flat sterns did not prove to be good sea boats under all conditions.

The power plant of the small launches built between 1876 and 1880 was a small coil boiler over a circular fire box and ash pit, the whole of which was enclosed by a cylindrical casing; the boiler was capable of making steam in only a few minutes. This was a single-cylinder engine of 3.5 inches bore and 7 inches stroke that developed about five horsepower. It should be remembered that the horsepower was developed from the energy of coal, which is different from the horsepower generated from gasoline or diesel fuel. The whole operation at that time was neat, simple, light, reliable and very economical.

One type of propeller used in the early Herreshoff launches and steamers was twenty-four inches in diameter and thirty-six inches in pitch, but Nathanael later designed a series of similar propellers in the early 1870s; they varied greatly in size, but not much in shape. The small launches generally used a two-bladed propeller. These were a true screw; they had the same pitch throughout the blade, and the blades were slightly concave on the pressure side both ways. When Nathanael Herreshoff was designing steam-driven craft, there were no commercial propellers made, so as long as the Herreshoff Manufacturing Company built steamers, it continued to make propellers of Nathanael's design in its own foundry.

During the American Civil War, Americans on both sides of the conflict endeavored to develop superior fighting ships. One of the attack vessels that was favored as an offensive weapon was the stealthy SPAR torpedo boat. In 1864 Union Navy Lieutenant William Cushing bravely faced a rain of Confederate shot to destroy the ironclad *Albemarle*, by means of a fast steam launch armed only with an explosive charge mounted on the end of a long pike, a SPAR torpedo.

The construction of steamers, it should be noted, was for many years Captain Nat's chief concern. His work at MIT, the Corliss shops and abroad had all been calculated to increase his knowledge in steam craft and make him more proficient in building them and their machinery.

In 1875, the U.S. Navy (Bureau of Ordnance) ordered the SPAR torpedo boat *Lightning* (Steam Launch No. 6), an open wooden launch, quarter decked fore and aft; she was launched May 1876 and her contract price was $5,000. This was the first torpedo boat purchased by the navy, although before this they had steam launches converted to torpedo boats. Herreshoff's *Lightning* was a long, narrow, double-ended launch, partly decked. She was fifty-eight feet long, and she carried two SPAR torpedoes. Her top speed was an impressive twenty-two knots, a record that had never been equaled by any boat of her length at that time.

On the trial trip of the *Lightning*, the designer was at the engine, showing that he could manage a steamer as well as a sailboat. Indeed, it was said that Captain Nat knew more about high-speed engines than anyone else in the country in those days.

Sometime before 1889, the *Lightning* was hauled up at the Naval Torpedo Station, worn out and no longer in service.

During the 1870s, experiments with high-speed torpedo boats such as Herreshoff's *Lightning* continued. There were many other builders of small, steam-propelled boats

The speedy double-ender steam SPAR torpedo boat the *Lightning* is seen at the Naval Torpedo Station at Goat Island in Newport Harbor, Rhode Island. *Courtesy Herreshoff Marine Museum.*

A U.S. Navy steam launch with sun shield in folded position; thirty-three feet long, nine feet draft, four feet two inches abeam, circa 1878. *Courtesy Herreshoff Marine Museum.*

in Europe and England. Among the several of the most successful in England were Thornycroft and Yarrow. Thornycroft built some of the first fast launches, and Yarrow specialized in high-speed steamers and other light craft. However, these other early torpedo boats all had heavy fire tube boilers and rather heavy hulls, so they were not as fast as the torpedo boats and launches being designed at the same time by the Herreshoffs in Bristol.

THE *VISION*

Buoyed by the success of the *Lightning*, the Herreshoff Manufacturing Company built a trial horse for a new type of coil engine. The *Vision*, as she was called, was extremely fast and brought international attention to the Bristol firm.

For an early trial run in November 1877, a group of U.S. government agents were invited to participate. After the guests had stepped aboard the narrow craft, James Herreshoff (brother of J.B. and Captain Nat) at the controls gunned the boat to life; she leapt to an almost instant fifteen knots, pushing the guests into their seats. They left the test ride sore of behind but impressed.

The *Vision* moved as fast as the *Lightning*, and she could be armed to work as either a torpedo boat or a gunboat. The U.S. Navy, as it turned out, was not interested, but the navies of foreign governments were.

THE *ESTELLE* AFFAIR

The impression of the *Vision* made that day was not lost on New York lawyer Herman Kobbe, who was also an unregistered agent for the insurgent government of Cuba. He immediately placed an order for a 120-foot steamer that could match the speed of the *Vision*. Kobbe put down cash to begin the work and promised a bonus for quick delivery of the boat, to be called *Estelle*, and to be a cargo carrier.

The *Estelle*, at 120 feet in length, 16 feet abeam, was too big to be built at the Bristol boatyard, so the hull construction was contracted to Job Terry's boatyard in Fall River, Massachusetts. When the hull was completed, John Brown used one of his 40-foot steamers to tow the *Estelle* to Bristol where the engine, boiler and other marine equipment were installed.

It was known that the *Estelle* was destined for use in the Caribbean Sea, and it was later learned that Kobbe had contracted for the fast boat on behalf of a group of Cuban gunrunning rebels.

Washington was keeping an eye on Cuba, and was also watching the progress of the *Estelle's* construction. In December 1877, the U.S. Revenue cutter *Dexter* arrived at Bristol, anchored in the harbor and kept watch on the Herreshoff dock and on the *Estelle*, which would soon begin her test runs. The *Dexter's* orders were not to let the boat leave the dock.

Shortly before Christmas 1877, the *Estelle*, with armed government agents from the *Dexter* aboard, made her trial run from Bristol to Brenton's Reef Light Ship and about sixty miles beyond into the Atlantic, before returning; the total elapsed time of the run was about six hours.

The Spanish gunboat the *Estelle* at the State Street Custom House dock; 120 feet long, 16 feet abeam, circa May 1877. *Courtesy Herreshoff Marine Museum.*

The owners were represented by Kobbe and a rough-looking Spaniard who was to operate the boat upon acceptance. The *Estelle*, which made a better speed than her contracted sixteen knots, was accepted by the owner's representatives and was paid for. She was then immediately seized by U.S. Treasury Department agents, and then secured at the Bristol Wharf. Part of her engine was taken as insurance that she would not leave.

The *Estelle* spent considerable time in government custody. In June 1878 she was released to Kobbe, who sold her to a man in Washington, D.C. The *Estelle*'s new owner employed her as a mail carrier and ultimately as a towboat at the mouth of the Mississippi, where she was known as the fastest tug in the area.

THE *STILETTO* AND OTHER STEAMERS

One of the earliest Herreshoff steamers to make a name for itself was the *Stiletto*, which created a sensation in 1885.[10] She was a long narrow craft, so promising in her speed trials that her captain sought out the *Mary Powell* on the Hudson and challenged her to a race. The *Mary Powell* had long been known as the fastest steamboat in this country,

After severely whipping the *Mary Powell*, the *Stiletto* beat the *Atalanta* in a New York Yacht Club regatta on June 11, 1885, with a record of twenty-nine miles in one hour and seventeen minutes. *Courtesy* Leslie's Illustrated Newspaper.

but the *Stiletto* kept on even terms with her, and at the end of the course she ran across the bow of her big rival. The speed of this audacious little vessel pleased U.S. Navy officials, and she was eventually purchased by the government for use in torpedo boat experiments.

In the *Frank Leslie Newspaper* report of the *Mary Powell* and *Stiletto* race dated June 20, 1885, the writer describes the *Stiletto* thus:

> The *Stiletto* *is a diminutive boat, only ninety-five feet long over all, with a water-line length but ninety feet, and a beam width of eleven. Her stern declines into almost as narrow a line as her bow. She was built by Herreshoff, the blind boat-builder of Bristol. Mr. Herreshoff may sell the* Stiletto *to some wealthy person who wants a fast boat, or perhaps he will offer her for naval service as a torpedo-boat. She shoots along without any other noise than is made by cleaving the water. Her boiler is a beehive coil, with the fire directly under it. The builder claims that it cannot explode; but even if it could, the danger would not be great, as it never contains more than a gallon of water at a time. The* Stiletto *can carry 200 pounds of steam.*

The following document addressed to Commander C.F. Goodrich, USN, stationed at the Naval Torpedo Station in Newport, Rhode Island, is logged as document #592 in the archives of the U.S. Naval Undersea Warfare Center, received on May 28, 1888, as "Authorizing the acceptance of the Stiletto."

> *Navy Department Washington,*
> *May 25, 1888*
> *Sir:*
> *You are hereby authorized and directed to accept delivery from the Herreshoff Manufacturing Company, of Bristol, R.I., of the vessel known as the "Stiletto" intended for use as a torpedo boat, and which has been purchased by authority of an act of Congress. After receiving the vessel you will, until further instructed, take proper care and custody of the same.*
> *A public bill, in triplicate, for the amount of the purchase money, viz.: $25,000, has been forwarded to Mr. John B. Herreshoff, treasurer of said Company, with the request that, after the triplicates shall have been duly receipted, he will cause the same to be handed to you. He has also been informed that you are authorized to receive the vessel and that paymeny [sic] of said bill will be made by the Pay Officer at the Station.*
>

> *Very respectfully,*
> *(signed) W.A. Whitney*
> *Secretary of the Navy*
>

Among the other notable speedy steam yachts of the Herreshoffs are the *Now Then, Say When* and *One Hundred*, all built primarily for their speed qualities; and the *Henrietta* and the 112-foot-6-inch *Vamoose*, the latter ordered by William Randolph Hearst. The *Vamoose* was called the fastest steam yacht in the world, and it is certain that she was at

Herreshoff's *Stiletto*, purchased by the U.S. Navy in 1887, was the first American torpedo boat capable of launching self-propelled torpedoes. *Courtesy United States Navy*.

The *Stiletto* is seen on parade in New York with the Atlantic fleet. Designated Wooden Torpedo Boat No. 1, a torpedo tube was mounted in the *Stiletto*'s bow. The navy conducted torpedo firing experiments in the Sakonnet River, off the shore of Tiverton, Rhode Island. *Courtesy United States Navy*.

Here the *Stiletto* is seen going at top speed firing a Howell torpedo from her port launcher. *Courtesy United States Navy.*

least one of the very fastest. Efforts were made time and again to race her against the speedy *Norwood*, but the match never occurred. Probably if she were beaten, Captain Nat would have stopped work on his sailing craft long enough to attempt the construction of a steamer that would be unquestionably the fastest steam yacht afloat.

Captain Nat's years of study on the subject were supplemented by several years of valuable experience when the government stationed a staff of officers at the Herreshoff works for the purpose of experimenting with high-speed machinery. No other firm in the country was making a specialty of that line of production at the time. Chief Engineer Benjamin F. Isherwood and a number of naval colleagues were at Bristol intermittently for four years, studying compound and triple expansion engines, the arrangement with the Herreshoffs amounting practically to a partnership between them and the Navy Department. The government furnished the expert knowledge required for the investigations, and the Herreshoffs supplied the shops and the other requisite facilities. There can be no doubt of the value to the younger Herreshoff of these years of association with the government experts. He had already become a master mechanic with few equals, and the hints he received in the course of his intimate acquaintance with the experienced investigators from Washington left him superior, in his own particular line, to any other American boat builder. It is no wonder, when we consider his natural genius, that his steam craft have proved to be the speediest vessels of their kind for the times.

Building the *Vamoose* in the north shed, 1891. *Courtesy Herreshoff Marine Museum.*

The *Vamoose* was built for William Randolph Hearst in 1891. She was built for speed; comfort was of secondary importance. Her huge quadruple-expansion steam engine turned a fifty-two-inch diameter propeller that drove her to a reported top speed of twenty-seven miles per hour. *Courtesy Herreshoff Marine Museum.*

The USS *Porter* (TB-6). The *Porter*, built in 1895, distinguished herself as a courageous fighting ship during the Spanish-American War. *Author's collection.*

The U.S. Navy's first all-steel, seagoing torpedo boat, the *Cushing*. Built in 1886, her lines are based on the *Stiletto* model. Her protected deadlights visible in her bulwarks are a feature carried over from the *Stiletto*. *Courtesy United States Navy*.

The USS *Porter* (TB-6). The *Porter*, built in 1895, distinguished herself as a courageous fighting ship during the Spanish-American War. *Courtesy United States Navy*.

The USS *Morris* (TB-14). The *Morris*, built in 1896, is seen here underway in Narragansett Bay. She successfully operated throughout her career at the Naval Torpedo Station as an experimental and training platform for launching torpedoes. *Courtesy United States Navy.*

The USS *Talbot* (TB-15). The *Talbot* and the *Gwin* (TB-16) were the smallest of the Herreshoff torpedo boats; they were assigned mostly to patrolling home waters. *Courtesy United States Navy.*

HERRESHOFF YACHTS

Some of the Herreshoff-built torpedo boats and others built by competing American yards took part in the war with Spain, but their use was mostly inconsequential to the effort. The boats were not assigned to missions to which they were best suited—swift attack and picket duty. Most often they were dispatched to patrol and carrier duty; their bunker capacity was too small to allow long periods at sea (frequent refueling was required), and they were too fragile for direct head-to-head combat with larger vessels.

The early torpedo boats did, however, provide valuable experience to future designers and builders. The development of the modern destroyer and torpedo technology can be laid directly to the first fledgling fleet of American torpedo boats.

CHAPTER 15

FOREIGN GOVERNMENT CRAFT

THE VEDETTE BOATS

Between 1878 and 1880, the Herreshoffs attempted to break into the booming torpedo boat market. They produced five double-ended, whale-backed, highly maneuverable craft to be armed with SPAR torpedoes. These boats were based on the *Lightning* model. For several years until 1885, the Herreshoffs built high-speed launches of forty to fifty feet for both the French and English governments. This class of boat was known as the Vedette class. In the building of fast craft for foreign navies, the Herreshoffs had no peer.

Of the four Vedette boats built for the U.S. Navy, two were to be carried aboard the *Maine* and two aboard the *Texas*. It was originally intended that the Vedette boats be carried on the decks of battleships. However, carrying such large and unwieldy things on the decks of ships proved to cause problems, and the plan was largely abandoned in nearly all navies.

The greatest speed ever obtained by a steam-propelled vessel, considering the size, is undoubtedly that reached by the Herreshoff Vedette boats built for the British navy. They were required to steam fourteen knots, and actually steamed fifteen and one-eighth knots. The success of these boats is due partly to the lightness of their construction and consequent moderate displacement.

BRITISH TORPEDO BOATS

Hull #44 was completed in July 1878 as a demonstration prototype. It was a very sophisticated war machine for the day. This vessel was bought on speculation by Mr. George R. Dunnell of London. The fifty-nine-foot double ender was taken to England by J.B. and Captain Nat, and demonstrated to the Royal Navy on the iced River Thames. She was subsequently purchased for the Royal Navy at the instigation of Chief Constructor Nathaniel Barnaby and thoroughly evaluated.

PERUVIAN TORPEDO BOATS

Hull #s53, 55 and 60 were open-decked double enders. Only #53 was 59 feet in length, 7 feet abeam and 5 feet draft. The other two were slightly smaller at 56 feet in length, 6

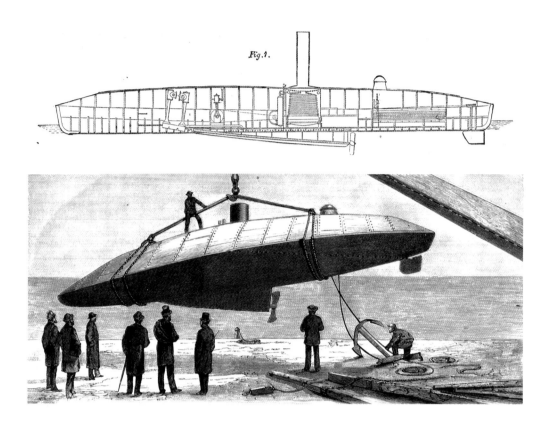

The British SPAR torpedo boat hull #44 was called "the coffin" by her crew; she was completed in July 1878. *Author's collection.*

The Spanish gunboat the *Clara*; 140 feet long, 9-foot draft, 9 feet abeam, circa May 1878. *Courtesy Herreshoff Marine Museum.*

A SPAR torpedo boat of the type built for the Peruvian navy, circa 1870. *Courtesy Herreshoff Marine Museum.*

feet 6 inches abeam and 4 feet 7 inches draft. The boiler and machinery were mounted aft and the driving screw, 33½ inches diameter, was mounted forward of amidships. These craft were built in four sections for easy transport and reconstruction on the West Coast.

Hull #53 was probably the vessel named *Republica* in the Peruvian navy. She and hull #55 saw action in the so-called Nitrate War between Chile, Peru and Bolivia during 1879–81.

Hull #60 was never delivered to Peru. She was left on the Herreshoffs' hands at the conclusion of the South American war and never found a buyer. It appears the U.S. government blocked delivery of this vessel just as the proposed Peruvian purchase of Ericsson's torpedo boat destroyer was blocked. The final resting place of hull #60 was in the open on Herreshoff's Point Pleasant Farm. The vessel was a neighborhood curiosity as she slowly deteriorated, lasting until about 1910. Surely, her longevity was a silent tribute to the materials and craftsmanship that produced her.

RUSSIAN TORPEDO BOATS

Hull #64 was a fifty-nine-foot double ender with a compound condensing two-cylinder engine. Her hull was double cedar wood built up at the end to accommodate four SPAR torpedoes, one on each quarter. The last of Herreshoff's double enders, nothing further is known of this craft. It is assumed that she was never commissioned as an operational boat after running trials.

During the winter of 1915, while Nathanael was in Bermuda, John negotiated with the Russian government for a number of high-speed seagoing torpedo boats. The deal with Russia was the biggest ever signed by John and the largest contract ever consigned to the Herreshoff boatyard. John knew this contract would garner work from other foreign governments that were arming against the Imperial German submarine threat.

Herreshoff's Russian SPAR torpedo boat hull #64. This line illustration clearly shows three of the four SPAR torpedoes this steam launch was designed to carry. *Courtesy* Scientific-American.

However, when Nathanael heard about the deal from his brother, he was not impressed. John told Nathanael the transaction was practically complete; it only needed his signature. Russian money was deposited, and construction was ready to begin, but Nathanael put a stop to it; he reminded his brother of their original agreement that the cost of doing business would never exceed money on hand, and of their mutual dislike for doing business with government.

In January 1918, near the end of World War I, the U.S. Navy sought a vendor to build an aircraft that would be able to cross the Atlantic under its own power and go directly into action against the German U-boat menace. The Curtiss Aeroplane and Motor Company of New York, an aviation pioneer, was selected.

Curtiss, in turn, subcontracted the fuselage work of the first four NC (Navy-Curtiss) planes. The NC-4 work was subcontracted to the Herreshoff Manufacturing Company to build the fuselage in the same manner of construction the Herreshoffs were known to apply to their sailing craft. A wooden fuselage built just like a boat's hull was constructed at the Bristol yard in 1918; this may be the origin of the description of an airplane with pontoons as a "flying boat." The NC-4 was a four-engine biplane with a 126-foot wingspan. It was one of four large flying boats designed and constructed as NC-1, -2, -3 and -4.

Building seaplane hulls for the navy was not unusual for Herreshoff at the time. The company had already built twenty hulls of various types beginning in 1917. But the NC-4 hull was special: it was big! Forty-five feet long and ten feet abeam, it had to be especially strong to withstand the impacts of landing and taking off at sea. It also had to be light and watertight.

To accomplish the contract specifications, a double layer of Sitka spruce planking fastened with copper was laid at opposing forty-five-degree angles from a Sitka spruce keel. Between the planking, Herreshoff's carpenters stretched a layer of muslin in marine glue. When completed, it weighed only 2,800 pounds.

Although the war had ended by the time the NC planes were ready to fly, the navy still wanted to test the theory that planes could fly across the Atlantic.

Because of damage from storm and fire, all of the NC planes except the NC-4 succumbed to mechanical problems of one sort or another and never completed the transatlantic flight. The NC-2 was salvaged to repair the NC-1, and its remainder became spare parts for the NC-4.

In 1919, the navy's NC-4 and a crew of six made the first successful transatlantic flight. It took some three weeks, May 8–27, to accomplish that. Humans had only taken wing in airplanes less than twenty years earlier, and Lindbergh's solo Paris flight was still eight years away.

The Navy-Curtiss flying boat NC-4. The U.S. Navy contracted the Curtiss aviation company to build four flying boats. Because the government contract called for delivery of all four airplanes in a short period of time, the Curtiss Company subcontracted the hulls to four different boatyards. *Author's collection.*

The NC-4 flying boat is one of the tangible symbols of aviation's historic development, both a harbinger of change and one of the sparks of the aerial revolution. Her epic transoceanic journey during the period of May 8–27, 1919, marked the first time an aircraft conquered the forbidding Atlantic. *Author's collection.*

Copyrighted by The International Film Service

Luckily, the contract to build the NC-4 hull was awarded to the Herreshoff Manufacturing Company. Only the NC-4 survived the flight to Europe and she is preserved at the National Museum of Naval Aviation at Pensacola.

This is a tourist snapshot of the NC-4 on the grounds of the Washington Monument in June 1923. The flying boat was on display during the Shrine convention. *Author's collection.*

The Herreshoff Manufacturing Company built ten F5L flying boat hulls in 1902. *Courtesy United States Navy.*

In the foreground is one of ten Herreshoff-built Curtiss H-16 flying boat hulls built in 1902. This circa 1918 U.S. Navy photo also shows a Curtiss HS-1L on the seaplane apron in the center distance at the Naval Air Station, Pensacola, Florida. *Courtesy United States Navy.*

The Herreshoff Manufacturing Company built ten sturdy lightweight hulls for the Curtiss H-16 flying boat using the same structural principles as their earlier steam launches. Circa 1922. *Courtesy United States Navy.*

Speed for Victory

Author's collection.

CHAPTER 17
TRANSITIONS

After the death of John Brown, the company's founder, in 1915, the company slipped into serious financial difficulties. Nathanael carried on the management of the yard, but he did not like to conduct business. In 1916, the company was taken over by a syndicate of wealthy yachtsmen. The boatyard struggled along until 1924, when it was put up for auction.

Part of the facilities was purchased by Rudolf F. Haffenreffer, who began to direct the yard's activities. Haffenreffer associated with the most notable yachtsmen in the country and surrounded himself in his yacht building activities with successful designers and skilled craftsmen who grew up in the Herreshoff guild of craftsmanship.

HAFFENREFFER MANAGEMENT

Under Haffenreffer's management the fame and respect that had grown for sixty years, influenced by the Herreshoff brothers, continued. For the races in 1930, the *Enterprise* designed by W. Starling Burgess and the *Weetamoe* designed by Clinton H. Crane were conceded to be faster than the other contenders; the other two 1930 contenders, built elsewhere, were fitted with many pieces of hardware designed and made in Bristol. The *Enterprise* was the selection of the committee to defend the Cup. She easily won four straight races with Lipton's *Shamrock V*, thereby adding more laurels to the Herreshoff name.

At no time during the history of the Herreshoff Manufacturing Company was its influence upon design and methods of construction matched by any competing American or international yacht builder. The variety of models, the physical equipment, the facilities for repairs and overhauling, the complete stock of materials, the convenience of approach to the docks and marine railways, the forge and foundry, machine and paint shops, sail, rigging and SPAR lofts all met the demands of the modern yachtsman, whether he owned power or sail, whether he owned a seagoing steam yacht or a modest 12½-footer.

For a great many years, all boats constructed were built using only designs prepared in the Herreshoffs' drafting rooms. However, when Rudolf F. Haffenreffer took control of the yard, he offered designers and marine architects, not connected to the company, the opportunity of having boats constructed from their plans.

The Haffenreffers made extensive improvements to the Herreshoff plant; Rudolf's active interest in the business and the fact that he had about him men who were responsible for the unquestioned leadership of Herreshoff boats during the period of his stewardship assured the world that the old Bristol art would not be forgotten, but would be carried on to even greater distinction.

Between 1940 and 1944, Bristol's fervent patriotism and the Herreshoff mastery of boat building came together in a production effort that contributed one hundred vessels to the Allied fleet and helped to lift the town out of an economic depression. When Rudolf F. Haffenreffer, as president, and his son Carl W., as general manager of the Herreshoff Manufacturing Company, secured a government contract for the boats, they put aside the sailing yachts that had made the yard famous. During the war years, a total staff of 2,000 Rhode Islanders became Herreshoff employees, but the workforce at any one time numbered about 450. The output of military craft that met Bristol Harbor from Herreshoff's construction shops numbered two 130-foot minesweepers, four 97-foot minesweepers, twenty-eight 71-foot patrol torpedo boats, twenty-two 103-foot troop transports, eight 85-foot Army Air Force rescue boats and thirty-six 83-foot rescue boats.

When the last of the contracted military craft sailed out of Bristol Harbor on November 24, 1944, Rudolf Haffenreffer proudly announced that no other shipyard in America or the world could turn out finer vessels.

At the end of the war, the Haffenreffers, who had owned the yard since 1924, assumed the end of the era of luxury yachts had passed; with no major contracts to fill, layoff letters went out to employees.

The historic boatyard tried its hand at making fiberglass dinghies and fulfilled a navy contract for life rafts. In the summer of 1945, all construction ceased, and the waterfront construction shops were torn down.

Rudolf F. Haffenreffer, president of the Herreshoff Manufacturing Company and builder of the 1930 W. Starling Burgess–designed J-class Cup defender *Enterprise*, hosted a challenger and defender clambake at his Bristol Mount Hope Farm residence. Seated in the front row of the gathering are (left to right) Harold S. Vanderbilt, owner and helmsman of the *Enterprise*; Rudolf F. Haffenreffer; and Sir Thomas Lipton, owner of the *Shamrock V*.

HERRESHOFF YACHT-DROME from the air . . . finest storage facilities in America, covering total area of 63,000 square feet, minimum headroom 19 feet. New, all-steel building at left offers 45,000 square feet clear storage space . . . 450 feet long, 102 feet wide, clear span. Building on right has headroom of 24 feet.

Herreshoff

MODERN FACILITIES FOR COMPLETE
WINTER-SERVICE

MR. E. D. Wright, of the Bureau for the Prevention of Explosion and Fire on Motor Yachts, recently made the following report to insurance companies: "I found the Herreshoff yard in perfect order, in fact, the best kept and cleanest plant I have ever had the pleasure of inspecting. . . . The yacht storage plant, to which has just been added a new all-steel shed, is swept absolutely clean. Also, buckets of sand are hung from the beams overhead, alongside the yachts, so that a man working on a boat can . . . at the least fire . . . pull the bucket up to him without delay, or, if a fire occurs outside the yacht while working on the bottom, the pail is within easy reach. . . . As Underwriters, I think if you were to go through the Herreshoff plant it would give you the same satisfaction that it did me. . . . For Winter Yacht Storage, I consider it one of the best risks we have."

EXPERIENCED yachtsmen immediately recognize the economy of winter storage in our Yacht-Drome with its scientific lighting and controlled ventilation. Protection under roof at the Herreshoff yard reduces maintenance costs to a minimum, permits work to be done at any time, regardless of weather or season and provides a year 'round showroom where yachts for sale can be seen at their best . . . a valuable aid to selling at a favorable price.

A Complete Service — Reasonable Rates

Yacht-Drome rates are based on floor area occupied, i.e., O.A.L. (including bowsprit or pulpit unless removed) x max. beam x $.20 for power yachts (or $.24 for sail and auxiliary yachts).

Write for illustrated booklet, "When Winter Comes", describing Herreshoff Winter-Service.

HERRESHOFF MANUFACTURING CO., BRISTOL, RHODE ISLAND

Author's collection.

CHAPTER 18

GLEANINGS

In this chapter are selected quotes garnered from nineteenth-century editions of the *Bristol Phoenix* as they refer to the Herreshoff Manufacturing Company or the Herreshoff family.

FEBRUARY 3, 1883. SIX VESSELS IN CONSTRUCTION.

The Herreshoff Manufacturing Co., has six vessels in process of construction, four steam propellers, and two sailing vessels. One of the steamers is a nondescript and is intended to be one of the fastest vessels afloat. Instead of ballast, this steamer has several thousand pounds of lead in a section, or sections of her keel. Business is booming at the boat building works.

APRIL 14, 1883. USN TORPEDO STATION VISITORS.

A board of steam engineers consisting of Chief Engineers Isherwood, Zeler, and Allen, from the United States Navy, with two assistants, is expected to visit the Herreshoff Mfg. Co's Works soon to superintend a series of experiments with the engine of the steam yacht Permelia, *which was launched on the 7th inst.*

APRIL 14, 1883. SUCCESSFUL LAUNCHINGS.

At the Herreshoff Mfg. Co's Works on Saturday last, there were two successful launching of vessels, the steam yacht Permelia *and the cutter* Consuelo. *The* Permelia *is 100 feet in length, by 12½ feet in width; engine 300-horsepower. The* Consuelo *was built for Mr. N.G. Herreshoff, she is 32 feet in length, about 8 foot beam, and 6½ feet in depth of hold, the ballast is of lead, in sections of her keel, and is 13,400 pounds in weight. Her interior is finished in the most elegant manner.*

Another steam yacht, called the Gov. Hamilton *was launched Monday morning. The* Gov. H. *is 76 feet in length, by 12½ feet in width, and has an engine of 100-horse power. She is intended to be used in the oyster culture in the head waters of Chesapeake Bay. The steam yacht* Orienta, *built here last season, has received a new engine and sailed for New York Saturday, whence she is soon to make a southern trip.*

JULY 28, 1883. THE HERRESHOFF STEAM YACHT WALKS AWAY FROM THE *ATALANTA*.

Jay Gould's happiness over the speed of his steam-yacht Atalanta, *in her brushes with Mr. Jaffray's steam-yacht* Stranger, *has been suddenly dashed. Before his boat had gone far on her run to Irvington, the bold pirate of Wall Street made out a craft on his weather quarter that seemed gliding after the* Atalanta *with intent to overhaul her. He however had a good start and sang out to the captain to keep his eye on the little stranger—not Mr. Jaffray's however.*

And it was not long before the strange boat came up abreast of the Atalanta, *and Jay was able to make out the mystical number "100" on her. Before long he was not only able to see the broadside of the "100" but in a little while he had a good view of her stern, whereon the figures were imprinted, and after a little while disappeared, as the "100" left the* Atalanta *which was carrying every pound of steam that could be carried without putting Jay Gould on the safety valve. Mr. Gould reached Irvington out of humor that evening.*

What of the mystic boat?

It is the latest production of the Herreshoff Manufacturing Company and is called "100." She is without a doubt the most wonderful yacht of her size for speed in this or any other country. Her length is 100 feet, with an extreme width of 12½ feet. The marvelous thing about her is her engine, which develops nearly 400 horsepower, giving her a speed of 19½ miles an hour. She beat the Atalanta *easily.*

AUGUST 18, 1883. SALE OF THE *100*.

Mr. J.B. Herreshoff's new steam yacht "100" was sold last week to Mark Hopkins, Esq., of St. Clair, Michigan. Monday morning she sailed for the home of her new owner, via the Hudson River, Erie Canal and Lake Erie. Undoubtedly she is the fastest steam yacht afloat.

OCTOBER 6, 1883. CAPT. NAT'S NEW HOUSE.

Mr. Nathaniel G. Herreshoff has a large two-story dwelling house, with large piazza and cupola, nearly completed on the south side of a continuation of Walley Street, west of Hope Street, which commands a fine and unobstructed view of the harbor, bay and neighboring islands. Mr. John Slade is the builder.

DECEMBER 29, 1883. HERRESHOFF-DEWOLF NUPTIALS.

Herreshoff-DeWolf, in this town, Dec 26th, at St. Michael's Church, by the Rev. George L. Locke, Nathaniel [sic] Green Herreshoff and Clara Anna, eldest daughter of the late A. Sydney DeWolf, all of Bristol.

Mr. Nathanael G. Herreshoff was presented with an elegant reclining chair on Saturday last, by Mr. A.S. Almy, in behalf of the foremen and employees of the Herreshoff Mfg. Co.

APRIL 7, 1888. US NAVY CONTRACT.

The Herreshoff Manufacturing Co., of this town has just received a contract from the United States government for the construction of a submarine torpedo boat at a cost of $82,750.

APRIL 28, 1888. STEAM YACHT *SAY WHEN.*

A new steam yacht built by the Messrs Herreshoff was launched from the boat works about 6:30 on Tuesday evening. The yacht was built for Mr. Norman L. Munro of New York and is 138 feet overall in length and 13 foot beam.

This is one of the finest yachts ever built in this or any other country. She is planked up from the water line in mahogany and is of the best possible workmanship.

Hundreds of our citizens witnessed the launching and cheered lustily when she glided down the ways into the water. Just as she started Mr. Munro's little daughter dashed a bottle of wine against her bow and christened the beautiful craft Say When. *Mr. Munro is also the owner of* Now Then. *The* Say When *is expected to do some very fast sailing and she is pretty as a picture.*

JUNE 2, 1888. THE *STILETTO.*

The navy torpedo boat launch Stiletto *that was built by Herreshoff Manufacturing Co., of this town, was put in commission at Newport on Monday last.*

SEPTEMBER 15, 1888. HERRESHOFF LAID TO REST.

The funeral of Mr. Charles Frederic Herreshoff was solemnized from his late residence Tuesday forenoon, Rev. George L. Locke officiating, assisted by Bishop Howe. The singing was by a select choir. There was a very large attendance of relatives and friends of the deceased. The remains were taken to Providence on the 12:42 train for interment.

DECEMBER 15, 1888. THE *SAY WHEN'S* BOILER BLOWS.

Saturday morning the steam yacht Say When *started out for a trial trip and about 10 o'clock, when off Bristol Ferry and ready to enter on her course a pipe in her coil boiler exploded and the force of the escaping steam blew out the fire, ashes, coal, etc., into the boiler room badly burning and scalding the two firemen, Charles Newman and George Horton.*

Mr. Newman was so seriously injured that he was immediately conveyed to the Rhode Island Hospital at Providence. His hands and face were terribly injured. Mr. Horton was taken to his home in this town and immediately received medical aid.

Mr. N.G. Herreshoff, who was on board the yacht at the time of the accident was landed at once and telephoned to Fall River for the tugboat T.M. Brown to steam to the Ferry to render assistance.

The steam tug was soon at the scene. The Say When *was towed to the Herreshoff Manufacturing Co.'s wharf.*

MAY 11, 1889. PERMISSION GRANTED.

[The Bristol Town Council] voted, that the Herreshoff Manufacturing Co., be and they are hereby authorized to proceed with concreting the sidewalk in front of their construction shops.

AUGUST 17, 1889. AFTER VACATION STARTUP.

The Herreshoff Manufacturing Co's Works, after a three weeks vacation, started up again Monday morning. They will build a 23-foot steam launch for the seal fisheries in Alaska.

DECEMBER 24, 1892. A CUP DEFENDER CONTRACT.

The Herreshoff manufacturing Company of this town has received an order, given by a New York Syndicate, for a steel boat of the required size, as a defender of the America's Cup and will soon commence its construction.

Mr. J.B. Herreshoff is quoted as saying, "The company has contracted to build a cup defender, and the contract is made with Mr. Archibald Rogers of New York as the head of the syndicate. We do not know who the other gentlemen are, All our dealings have been with Mr. Rogers. The boat will be built of steel and set up in the same shop soon as the Carroll 84-footer can be got out of the way. The material is contracted for some of it will be here next week, and all of it within a fortnight.

"In view of the importance of the contest for the cup, and the need of keeping as much as possible about it secret until the challenger is under way, I trust you will see the impossibility of my giving further information about the boat. She is ordered and we will build her as fast as we can build her."

Mr. Oliver Iselin, the former owner of the crack sloop Titania, *says, "The Herreshoffs are, without doubt, the leading yacht designers in this country and they will undoubtedly turn out a boat fast enough to keep the cup, so I fail to see the necessity of another boat. A cup defender would probably cost about $75,000, which would make it an expensive plaything for one season."*

JANUARY 14, 1893. A GOVERNMENT ORDER.

An order was received by the Herreshoff Manufacturing Co., of this town; last week, from the Assistant Secretary of the Navy, Mr. Soley, for a steam launch twenty-eight feet in length, to be used at the Massachusetts Nautical Training School in connection with the training ship Enterprise.

The government has experimented a great deal with steam launches but none have stood the test as well as those made by Herreshoff.

MARCH 25, 1893. A BUSY WEEK.

Here vessels have been launched from the Herreshoff's establishment this week. Monday morning the 90-foot steam yacht Kalolah *glided down the ways from the shop into the water. She is known by her builders as No. 173. Immediately after the* Kalolah *was afloat the 28-foot U.S. government steam launch was put into the water. This launch is to be sent to the U.S. Navy yard in Portsmouth, N.H., to be used as a tender for the ship* Enterprise. *Tuesday morning the steam yacht* Louise, *built for C.H. Hayden of Cleveland was launched. The three were all placed in the water without any accident worth mentioning.*

APRIL 15, 1893. THE *NAVAHOE*.

The past week has been a busy one for Bristol yachtsmen in general, but especially for patrolman Wilcox at the Herreshoff Works. When it became generally known that the Navahoe *had made a preliminary trial trip, newspapermen, photographers, and the curious class, flocked to Bristol in squads to get a glimpse of the first of the big single stickers.*

Boston yachtsmen seem very much exercised over the fact that the Herreshoffs did not build a fin keel as they were the originators of that style of racing machine. However the great building firm does not believe fin keel style of boat is practical beyond the 46-foot class. As Mr. John B. Herreshoff said, "We put bibs and pinafores on babies and young children, but older people require something different."

MAY 19, 1893. 50TH WEDDING ANNIVERSARY.

The sons and daughters of Mr. and Mrs. Charles Frederick Herreshoff held a grand reception on Tuesday afternoon from 2 to 5 o'clock, at the residence of Mrs. Chesebro, Hope Street, for the celebration of the 50th anniversary of their parents' wedding. Very many of our prominent citizens, as well as a goodly number from Providence and other towns and cities were present, including a large number of ladies.

Of [the couple's] *nine children, seven sons and two daughters, which they have been blessed, now all living, eight were present, as were also the wives of four sons, and five of their nine grandchildren. One son Mr. James B. Herreshoff, who resides in London, was unable to be present.*

Mr. and Mrs. Herreshoff were married in Boston, May 15, 1833, by Rev. M.J. Motte of that city. Mr. Herreshoff was born in Providence, and Mrs. Herreshoff, nee Miss Julia A. Lewis, was born in Boston. Mr. Herreshoff has resided in Bristol nearly all his life, his parents having moved from Providence to this town when he was an infant. After their marriage they resided on Poppasquash about 21 years, when they removed to their present family mansion, adjacent to which is the residence of their Daughter Mrs. Chesebro. The reception was one of rare enjoyment to all who participated.

MAY 20, 1893. THE *COLONIA*.

Monday evening a few minutes after seven o'clock the first of the four America-cup defenders, bearing the name Colonia, *was successfully launched from the Herreshoff Company's Yard in this town. There was only a small gathering of spectators to witness the launching as no public announcement had been made and the affair was without ceremony.*

The Colonia *is said to be the largest sloop ever built in this country. She is 126 feet overall, and the length of the water line 85 feet, draft about 16 feet. She is painted white with green underneath; she is a handsome vessel. The riggers commenced their labors Monday morning.*

JUNE 17, 1893. THE *COLONIA'S* TRIAL TRIP.

The Colonia, *the yacht built by the Herreshoffs for the Rogers syndicate, made a trial trip Monday; the wind was unfavorable but it was plainly demonstrated that she will be a very fast sailor.*

JULY 22, 1893. THE *VIGILANT* LEAVES BRISTOL.

The Cup defender Vigilant, *built by the Herreshoff Mfg. Co., sailed for New York last Tuesday night, having her owners and friends on board. It is expected that the vessel will make a fine record, and if chosen to defend America's Cup will "get there."*

OCTOBER 28, 1893. REDUCED WORK FORCE.

The Herreshoffs will start their shops next Monday with a reduced force. They have an order for a 110-foot steam yacht and they will also continue work on the 80-foot steam yacht for the president of the company, Mr. John B. Herreshoff.

MARCH 26, 1895. SAILS FOR THE NEW DEFENDER.

The sails of the new cup defender, which will be laid down in the large unoccupied room at the rubber works will be made of ramie cloth, a material manufactured from grasses that grow in Texas, and also in eastern countries. It is much lighter and tougher than cotton or linen duck and when wet is even stronger than when dry. In color the cloth is nearly white, shading a trifle on the yellow. The reporters of the metropolitan press will now have another place to storm but much good it will do them, for the room used in making the sails will be as carefully guarded as is the Herreshoff Works.

MAY 10, 1895. SPANISH TORPEDO BOATS.

It is said that the Herreshoffs have put in a bid to build six steel torpedo boats for the Spanish government. These boats are to be from 95 to 120 feet in length and have a speed of from 18 to 21 knots. They are to be used as patrol boats along the coast of Cuba.

JUNE 11, 1895. THE *VIGILANT* RETURNS TO BRISTOL.

Vigilant, *the ex Cup defender, arrived in Bristol early Saturday morning. She was towed into the harbor by the tug* Aeronaut *from New York. It is her first appearance in these waters in two years. Capt. Charles Barr is skipper of the* Vigilant *and he is on board in command. She has a crew of 30 men and 10 or 12 more are engaged which will make the full complement needed during the season. Her object in coming to Bristol now is to procure a centerboard, and yesterday morning she was towed out into the ship channel and anchored just north of Castle Island beacon in Bristol Harbor for the purpose of having the new center board hung.*

JULY 19, 1895. TUNING THE *DEFENDER.*

Defender *and* Colonia *sailed up from Newport yesterday and dropped anchor off Herreshoff's about two o'clock.* Defender's *trial with* Vigilant *off Newport Sunday demonstrated that* Defender *is much faster than the old champion is, and everybody is satisfied that the new racer will be a winner.* Defender *will be finished up, turned over to the syndicate, and taken to New York in time for the big races there off Sandy Hook on Saturday and Monday.*

SEPTEMBER 5, 1895. GREAT INTEREST IN *DEFENDER'S* HOMETOWN.

Bristol people are naturally much interested in the international yacht races, the first of which is to be sailed tomorrow. Many from this town will attend. Bulletins of the race will be received at the drug store of J.H. Young & Co., every half hour after the start tomorrow; neither Englishmen nor Americans are over sanguine as to the result of the contest, as everybody realizes that it will be a doughty struggle to the end.

There are those who are superstitious enough to say that Defender's *13 mishaps auger ill fortune for her, while others have faith in the old adage that a "bad beginning makes a good ending," and "there ye air." However, we are of the opinion that* Defender *will prove worthy of her name, and that the Cup, which was, so gallantly won from our English cousins in 1851 and has since been successfully defended in eight international races against the best boats that could be built in foreign countries, will remain on this side.*

SEPTEMBER 13, 1895. THE *DEFENDER* CAPTURES THE CUP.

America's Cup is safe for at least another year, but the fiasco, which brings about the result, is very unsatisfactory to all true sportsmen. Saturday's race was squarely won by Defender. *Tuesday's race was awarded* Defender *on a foul, after she had virtually won it by plainly showing her superiority over the Englishman, even in a crippled condition. In yesterday's race Lord Dunraven withdrew* Valkyrie *immediately after the start.* Defender *went over the course alone and was awarded three races and the Cup.*

Lord Dunraven does not claim that he was treated unfairly, but says he withdrew because of interference by the fleet of excursion steamers. He has laid himself open to the charge of not being a "dead game sport" and of being afraid of a crushing defeat yesterday in a strong breeze.

However, the Cup would have stayed here had three genuine races been sailed, Defender's *corrected time over the 30-mile course yesterday, sailing alone without special effort, 4 hours, 43 minutes, and 43 seconds, which is fast under the circumstances. Mr. N.G. Herreshoff arrived in Bristol this morning and has expressed himself disgusted with the fizzle. He naturally wanted to know just how badly* Defender *could beat* Valkyrie.

OCTOBER 27, 1895. U.S. NAVY TORPEDO BOATS.

Commander G.A. Converse, who is to superintend the construction of the two new torpedo boats at the Herreshoff Works, visited Bristol Saturday. He stated that the contracts for material had just been signed and that castings and material for the hulls are expected to begin arriving at the Herreshoff works in about three weeks. The Phenix [sic] Iron Works of Philadelphia and Nashua Iron Works of New Hampshire are the contractors.

NOVEMBER 8, 1895. FLORENCE DEWOLF'S MINIATURE VERSION OF *DEFENDER*.

The Kildee, *a 25 footer with 18 feet water line, was launched from the Herreshoff Works on Saturday. She was built for Miss. Florence DeWolf, sister of Mrs. N.G. Herreshoff, and is a pocket edition of* Defender, *being built on practically the same lines, even to her lead bulb. She was given a satisfactory spin on Sunday trying her speed against the* Edith M., *the later being sailed by Capt. Nat Herreshoff.*

MAY 19, 1896. NEW GOVERNMENT LAUNCH.

The new Government steam launch, which was put overboard at Herreshoff's yesterday, was given a trial trip in the harbor in the afternoon. James T. Robertson was the engineer, and Capt. Nat Herreshoff was at the helm. The launch is about 45 feet overall and 37 feet on the waterline. She is built of mahogany.

OCTOBER 3, 1896. WASHINGTON TRIP.

Mr. John B. Herreshoff, accompanied by his wife, started for Washington, D.C., Sunday night on business connected with the new torpedo boats for which bids are soon expected to be awarded by Secretary Herbert.

MARCH 6, 1897. TORPEDO BOAT ENGINES.

Work on torpedo boat No. 6 is being carried on each evening until 10 or 11 o'clock in order to get her ready for her official trials as soon as possible. Thus far the vessel has developed speed of 24½ knots under two boilers without carrying her full pressure of steam. As yet she has not been tried with three boilers. Torpedo boat No. 7, now being built at Herreshoff's will probably not be launched until spring, as she will be nearly completed before being put into the water.

JUNE 12, 1897. TORPEDO BOAT NO. 7 THE *DUPONT*.

The United States Torpedo boat No. 1 [Cushing] arrived here Saturday from Newport with officers to inspect the work on the torpedo boat Dupont which will have her trial trips in a few weeks. Torpedo boat No. 1 was formerly [assigned] on the Battleship Maine.

JUNE 19, 1897. THE TORPEDO BOAT NO. 6 THE *PORTER*.

The Honorable Theodore Roosevelt, acting Secretary of the Navy, has written a letter to Commander George A. Converse, congratulating him on the excellent results attained by the torpedo boat Porter, of which he was the inspector-in-charge for the navy department, as well as for the perfection of the torpedo boat's construction. The letter congratulates the contractors, the Messrs. Herreshoff and Lieutenant S.S. Wood, USN, the assistant inspector at the Herreshoff works.

For 80 years, the name "Herreshoff" has been closely linked with yachting. The Cup Defenders *Vigilant, Defender, Weetamoe, Resolute* and *Enterprise* were Herreshoff-built, and their hull plates were Tobin Bronze*, an exclusive Anaconda Alloy. The 1934 winner, *Rainbow*, shown here, was Tobin Bronze plated below the water line.

A 103-foot, APc Coastal Transport built by Herreshoff

IN PEACE OR WAR

Herreshoff builds with Rustproof Anaconda Metals

Herreshoff—widely known builder of America's Cup Defenders and currently building Mine-Sweepers, Motor Torpedo Boats (PT's), and Coastal Transports for the Navy—has been a consistent user of Anaconda Metals.

In APc Coastal Transports launched in large numbers from the Herreshoff yards, thousands of non-rusting Everdur* Screws were used for hull fastenings. Anaconda

Copper and Copper Alloys were employed extensively for brackets, struts and other marine hardware . . . for structural plate and pipe and tubing.

Owners of pleasure craft of the future will benefit from new production methods developed by our leading builders in supplying the large volume of construction needed by our armed forces.

*Tobin Bronze and Everdur Reg. U.S. Pat. Off.   48185

ANACONDA *Anaconda Copper & Brass*

THE AMERICAN BRASS COMPANY—General Offices: Waterbury 88, Connecticut
Subsidiary of Anaconda Copper Mining Co. • In Canada: ANACONDA AMERICAN BRASS LTD., New Toronto, Ont.

Author's collection.

CHAPTER 19

HERRESHOFF MARINE MUSEUM AND AMERICA'S CUP HALL OF FAME

After many years of planning, the Herreshoff Marine Museum opened its doors in 1977, on the same land and in the same buildings from which some of the world's most renowned vessels were designed, built and launched.

In gala ceremonies, the A. Sidney DeWolf Herreshoff Room, featuring an extensive collection of classic boats, steam engines, photographs and wide-ranging memorabilia, was formally dedicated in the former east storehouse of the Herreshoff Manufacturing Company at 18 Burnside Street, Bristol, Rhode Island.

The museum's virtual age is greater than its actual age. The museum effectually began in the old family home, Love Rocks, which Captain Nat built as his residence. In 1953, when the family sold the house, Captain Nat's son, Sidney, moved upward of six hundred models his father had made to an addition to his home and, with loving care, created a place for their preservation.

Between 1953, when he moved the models to his own home, and 1977, when he died, Sidney Herreshoff, on special occasions, opened the model room to visiting yachtsmen and naval design scholars.

After Sid's death, and following the purchase, in 1977, of a former Herreshoff Manufacturing building at 18 Burnside Street, the Herreshoff family, including Sid's widow Rebecca (Becky) Chase and their son Halsey, initiated a display gallery there, appropriately establishing a room of boats in honor of A. Sidney DeWolf Herreshoff.

Today, the Herreshoff most visible in preserving the family history is Halsey Chase Herreshoff, president of the museum. The Herreshoff Marine Museum preserves the legacy of the genius of the inventive family and the dedication of the many hundreds of men and women crafters who worked on this hallowed land beginning in 1865.

We can think of no finer place in the world to establish a shrine honoring the champions of the America's Cup than the place where so many were brought to life. The America's Cup Hall of Fame preserves and celebrates the unique accomplishments of the Herreshoffs and the many internationally distinguished yacht designers and helmsmen, and the related drama of the America's Cup races to educate and inspire.

To learn more about the Herreshoff Marine Museum and America's Cup Hall of Fame you are invited to visit the museum on the Internet at www.Herreshoff.org.

The gasoline launch *240* on the Thames River, New London, Connecticut, June 29, 1905. The *240* takes her name from her hull number, 240. She was built as a vehicle in which to test one of the few gasoline engines that Captain Nat designed. *Courtesy Herreshoff Marine Museum.*

Now fully restored, the *240* can be admired, up close, in the Herreshoff Marine Museum. *Courtesy Herreshoff Marine Museum.*

Captain Nat and Halsey. *Author's collection.*

Author's collection.

APPENDIX

The following is taken from a published town tax record titled "A list of Persons, Corporations, Companies, & Estates, as assessed in accordance with the town tax Bristol, R.I., 12th day of April, A.D. 1884."

Name	Description	Real	Personal	Total	Tax
Chesebro, Caroline L.	House and lot, east side Hope Street	$4,700		$4,700	$35.75
Herreshoff, Charles F. and wife	Homestead estate, east side Hope Street	$6,000			
Herreshoff, Charles F. and wife	House and lot, north of Hope Street	$1,700			
Herreshoff, Charles F. and wife	Personal		$300	$8,000	$60
Herreshoff, Charles F.	Personal		$10,000	$10,000	$75
Herreshoff, James B.	Personal		$3,200	$3,200	$24
Herreshoff, Charles F., Jr.	Personal		$1,500	$1,500	$11.25
Herreshoff, John B. and wife	House and lot, south side Burnside Street	$1,500			
Herreshoff, John B. and wife	House and lot, 30 Burton Street	$2,000			
Herreshoff, John B. and wife	House and lot, south side 36 Burton Street	$2,200			
Herreshoff, John B. and wife	House and lot, 8 Howe Street	$2,200			
Herreshoff, John B. and wife	House and lot, 5 Howe Street	$1,500			

APPENDIX

Name	Description	Real	Personal	Total	Tax
Herreshoff, John B. and wife	Three houses and lots, west side Howe Street	$4,500			
Herreshoff, John B. and wife	Personal		$5,000	$18,900	$141.75
Herreshoff, John B.	Lot and cellar, east side High Street, Howe Plat	$3,500			
Herreshoff, John B.	Two lots and house, west side Howe Street	$2,000			
Herreshoff, John B.	One house and lot, north side Smith Street	$3,000			
Herreshoff, John B.	One lot, west side Howe Street	$200		$8,700	$65.25
Herreshoff, Nathanael G.	Four lots land, cellar and house, west side Hope Street and north side Walley Street	$5,000			
Herreshoff, Nathanael G.	Personal		$10,000	55,000	$412.50
Herreshoff Mfg. Co.	Shore lot and buildings, etc., west side Hope Street	$14,000			
Herreshoff Mfg. Co.	Lot of land and buildings, south side Burnside Street	$6,000			
Herreshoff Mfg. Co.	Boats building in shops, steam engines, machinery, etc.	$25,000			
Herreshoff Mfg. Co.	Personal		$10,000	$55,000	$412.50
Herreshoff, Sarah, heirs of	Personal		$15,000	$15,600	$117.00
Herreshoff, Ann Frances	Farm on Pappoosesquaw Neck	$18,000			
Herreshoff, Julia A., wife of Charles F.	Right, title and interest to house and lot, corner of Thames and Oliver Streets	$1,000			
Herreshoff, Julia A., wife of Charles F.	House and lot, Hope Street, near Walley Street	$2,000		$3,000	$22.50

NOTES

Chapter 1

1. Karl Friedrich was born in Minden the same year the Seven Year's War Battle of Minden took place.

2. The Herreshoff family uses the modern spelling of his name, since it has appeared in several different forms in the past.

3. The Amber Room (Bernsteinzimmer in German) was located in the Catherine Palace outside St. Petersburg. It was dismantled and taken away by the Germans in World War II and has never been found. A reproduced version is now on display at the palace.

4. Karl Friedrich was well over six feet tall.

5. Minden is located in Westfalen (Westphalia in English).

6. Frederick the Great's actual first two names were Karl Friederich.

7. He was the consecrated bishop of the Eastern Episcopal Diocese in 1811, and chancellor of Brown University from 1815 to 1831.

Chapter 2

8. See Samuel Carter III, *The Boatbuilders of Bristol.*

Chapter 4

9. In the 1860s, the *Great Eastern* was the largest steel ship afloat. She began life in 1858 as the *Leviathan.* She was the only passenger ship large enough to carry the single length of cable needed to span the Atlantic. The *Great Eastern* weighed eighteen thousand tons and was seven hundred feet long and eighty-five feet wide.

Chapter 14

10. For an in-depth history of the *Stiletto*, see Richard V. Simpson, *Building the Mosquito Fleet.*

This 1893 stereoview card image shows the Cup defender *Vigilant* during the defender trials for the Goelet Cup in Newport, Rhode Island.

BIBLIOGRAPHY

Bains, Joseph J. *The Prudence Inn Land from Prudence Farm to Prudence Conservancy.* Privately published, 1997.

Blunt, White G.W. L. Francis Herreshoff Collection, Library, Mystic Seaport, CT.

Bray, Maynard, and Carlton Pinheiro. *Herreshoff of Bristol.* Brooklin, ME: Woodenboat Publications, 1989.

Bristol Phoenix. Selected news items, 1883–98.

Burnett, Constance Buel. *Let the Best Boat Win.* Boston: Houghton Mifflin Company, 1957.

Carter, Samuel, III. *The Boatbuilders of Bristol.* New York: Doubleday & Company, 1970.

Field, Edward. *State of Rhode Island, and Providence Plantations at the End of the Century: A History.* Boston: The Mason Publishing Co., 1902.

Frank Leslie's Popular Monthly 48 (July 1899).

Friedman, Norman. *U.S. Small Combatants.* Annapolis, MD: Naval Institute Press, n.d.

Grant, J.A. "Herreshoff SPAR Torpedo Boats." *Warship International* 15, no. 3 (1977).

Herreshoff, L. Francis. *Capt. Nat Herreshoff.* New York: Sheridan House, 1953.

———. *An Introduction to Yachting.* New York: Sheridan House, 1980.

Lippincott, Bertram. *Indians, Privateers, and High Society.* Philadelphia and New York: J.B. Lippincott Co., 1961.

Bibliography

Middleton, Alicia Hopton. *Life in Carolina and New England During the Nineteenth Century.* Privately published, 1929.

Palmieri, John. *The Clara Trilogy.* Classic Yacht Symposium Proceedings, 2005.

Pinheiro, Carlton J. *Bristol, Three Hundred Years.* Providence: Franklin Graphics, 1980.

———. *Recollections and Other Writings.* Bristol, RI: Herreshoff Marine Museum, 1998.

Simpson, Richard V. *The America's Cup Yachts: The Rhode Island Connection.* Charleston, SC: Arcadia Publishing, 1999.

———. *Bristol: Montaup to Poppasquash.* Charleston, SC: Arcadia Publishing, 2002.

———. *Building the Mosquito Fleet: The U.S. Navy's First Torpedo Boats.* Charleston, SC: Arcadia Publishing, 2001.

"Stiletto, The Swift." *Frank Leslie Illustrated Newspaper,* June 20, 1885.

Yachting. September 1934.

In this circa 1899 photo are seen four U.S. Navy torpedo boats in their slips at the Naval Torpedo Station on Goat Island in Newport Harbor. Left to right the boats are the *Winslow* and the Herreshoff-built *Stiletto, Morris* and the *Porter*. In the background are the Newport skyline and two New York excursion steamers of the Fall River Line, the *Pilgrim* (left) and the *Priscilla*.

ABOUT THE AUTHOR

Richard V. Simpson is a native Rhode Islander who moved to Bristol in 1960. During the decades of the America's Cup defenses in Rhode Island Sound, he was employed as a graphic designer at the Naval Supply Center and at the U.S. Naval Undersea Warfare Center (NUWC) in Newport; it was then that he first took notice of the yachts struggling for possession of the America's Cup.

One of his official duties was to research early torpedoes and torpedo firing platforms for technical manuals and to design educational displays and exhibits for public information. It was this research that brought him to the U.S. Naval Museum in Newport, and the Naval War College and NUWC libraries. While studying century-old documents, faded patent sketches, grainy photographs and bound copies of the weekly journal *Scientific American*, he "discovered" the relationship between the torpedoes developed and manufactured at the old Naval Torpedo Station on Goat Island in Newport Harbor and the early swift steam launches built for the U.S. Navy by the Herreshoff Manufacturing Company of Bristol.

This new insight regarding the Bristol firm prompted him to begin collecting written and graphic documentation about the Herreshoffs' speedy steam-driven yachts, military craft and their sleek and graceful sailing yachts. So large had his collection grown that when he retired from government service in 1996, he began organizing his material with the intent to write books on the subjects: *America's Cup Yachts: The Rhode Island Connection* was published in 1999, and *Building the Mosquito Fleet: The U.S. Navy's First Torpedo Boats* was published in 2001.

Since 1967, Simpson has published thirteen titles dealing with Rhode Island history. Beginning in 1985, he became a contributing editor for the national monthly *Antiques & Collecting Magazine*, in which over seventy-five of his articles have appeared. In 2006, he and associate Zsolt Orban produced a three-hundred-year historical documentary movie about Bristol, Rhode Island.

Other Books by Richard V. Simpson

A History of the Italian-Roman Catholic Church in Bristol, RI (1967)
Independence Day: How the Day is Celebrated in Bristol, RI (1989)
Old St. Mary's: Mother Church in Bristol, RI (1994)
Bristol, Rhode Island: In the Mount Hope Lands of King Philip (1996)
Bristol, Rhode Island: The Bristol Renaissance (1998)
America's Cup Yachts: The Rhode Island Connection (1999)
Building the Mosquito Fleet: The U.S. Navy's First Torpedo Boats (2001)
Bristol: Montaup to Poppasquash (2002)
Bristol, Rhode Island: A Postcard History (2005)
Narragansett Bay: A Postcard History (2005)

Books by Richard V. Simpson and Nancy J. Devin

Portsmouth, Rhode Island: Pocasset: Ancestral Lands of the Narragansett (1997)
Tiverton and Little Compton, Rhode Island: Pocasset and Sakonnet (1997)
Tiverton and Little Compton, Rhode Island: Volume II (1998)

Visit us at
www.historypress.net